BORN TO LEAD: AWAKENING THE LEADER WITHIN

Jacqueline Kaba-Harrison
Visionary Author

© 2022

ALL RIGHTS RESERVED. No part of this book may be reproduced in any written, electronic, recording, or photocopying without written permission of the publisher or author. The exception would be in the case of brief quotations embodied in the critical articles or reviews and pages where permission is specifically granted by the publisher or author.

Publisher: Touched by a Dove Publishing
Book Editor: Dana M. Hutchinson
Book Design and Layout: S. Michelle LeSuer
Cover Design: Tanisha Pettiford

Library of Congress Cataloging – in- Publication Data has been applied for.

ISBN: 978-1-7355336-7-4

PRINTED IN THE UNITED STATES OF AMERICA

CONTENTS

Foreword Precious Williams	1
Introduction: In The Beginning, A Leader Was Born Jacqueline Kaba-Harrison	7
I Am Leadership Jacqueline Kaba-Harrison	11
What the Enemy Meant for Evil, God Turned It for My Good Ebony Butler	19
Queen, Adjust Your Crown and LEAD Dr. Nakita Davis	33
BELIEVE in Your "Leadershipreneur" Abilities Sonya Davis	41
Lead and Leave Your Mark on the World Angela Lewis	55
What Doesn't Kill You … Rev. Keever Lernise Murdaugh	68
Resilience Against All Odds Keiaundria Ragland	80
The Road to CEO: Overcoming the Storm Natalie S. Williams, Esq.	90
Concluding the Whole Matter Jacqueline Kaba-Harrison	113

FOREWORD
PRECIOUS WILLIAMS

My Black Queens ... *Born to Lead* is a must-read if, you have ever failed, made a mistake, or allowed the opinions of others to stop you from achieving the dreams God placed in your heart. In this book, you will read eight amazing stories of Black women who, despite life's challenges, overcame the odds to become the leaders they are today. It didn't come easy, but I bet if you were to ask them if it was worth it, they wouldn't have wanted it any other way.

My sisters, what if I told you that you are not alone? Welcome and join the club! Allow me to remind you that you are human and are not defined by your past shortcomings as the co-authors weren't defined by theirs. The truth is, as Black women, life hasn't been easy. Some of us grew up wanting to be popular, to fit in, or not wanting to make waves. As a result, we turned into people pleasers who lost our voice. Since we did not fit the mold that society created, it forced us to hide from our pasts, only to present a perfectly crafted façade as opposed to walking in authenticity. We wouldn't have known what leadership looked like if it came and introduced itself.

Yet, as we matured, we discovered that those traits were not healthy and decided not to pass them on to our children. Also when we no longer saw our sisters as a threat, something began to change. We defiantly learned to love the skin we are in, accepted our calling, and our leadership journey was underway! You can't lead others if you don't see the quality trait in yourself. Leaders do not follow the pact. They do not put on false heirs. They also understand that mistakes and failures are crucial stepping stones to success. When we embrace our pasts – the good, the bad, and the ugly of it all, we adapt to a changing world and boldly step out in true acceptance of who and what God created us to be. We become stronger, courageous, apply wisdom, and don't mind going against the grain!

As leaders we must not allow society, family, and/or cultural norms dictate our value based on the color of our skin. It's encouraging when women who look like us tell about the challenges they faced head-on that lead them to success. It's also comforting to know that it's not just reserved for the hands of the wealthy and/or well-connected! Yes, what seems impossible becomes possible when we dare ourselves to lead, in spite of the adversities we face. This is why this book is so powerful! What you have in your hands right now, is a game-changer!

I was delighted to be asked to write the Foreword for *Born to Lead*! Why? Because its Visionary, Jacqueline Kaba-Harrison wanted to make sure that as sisters, we know that leadership is our birthright as shown by our mothers, grandmothers, and other powerful African American women in history. If our "Sheroes" could do it way back when, then we can too. Secondly, she's an unstoppable force for all women, especially Black women and whose mission is to provide the necessary resources for us to excel in leadership.

This book is not for everyone. No ma'am ... no sir! See, the Black Queens who will read this book will discover that she too, can lead after trauma, drama, or even after making bad decisions. She has decided that her past will no longer weigh down her present and future! The powerful co-authors in this book will confirm through their own experiences, that God is no respecter of person. What He did in and through their lives He can do in and through YOU!

Leadership is not a linear path. Like life, there will be curve balls, roller coaster rides, and things you will never see coming. As African American women, leading others can be a daunting task given your family, work, and personal commitments. However, GOD has equipped you to lead and to be a beacon light for others. It goes without saying that life would be easy if everything were perfect. But where is the challenge in that? Think back to a time when you thought you were not going to make it; or when you made a decision that should have been the end of you. But yet, you are still here. The lessons you learned and are still learning are priceless and now are helping others. That is what being born to lead is all about. Often times we lead from dark places by overcoming our trials and tribulations. We save others from making the same mistakes we made, while preparing them for those to come.

What would happen if as Black women we decided to re-imagine everything in our lives to what's possible from the inside out? What if we allowed ourselves permission to be great leaders, and to BOLDLY step into our greatness, the world be damned! It's no longer acceptable to be invited to party if we're not allowed to dance! Not only must we lead by example without fear, but we must also challenge those to whom dare us not. We must be prepared for when our number is called!

I am simply positing that it's time to restart the leadership conversation and begin to question why we're not seeing women who look like us in leadership positions. After reading the incredible stories in Born to Lead, you will be challenged to deal with the "elephant in the room" and begin having the tough conversations if you're not having them already.

For those women who are already in leadership roles, it's time to enhance your skills and pass them on to those in your sphere of influence who have not prepared themselves or have not been provided opportunities to lead. Jacqueline Kaba-Harrison wants every reader who picks up this book to know that they innately possess leadership qualities and to conduct themselves accordingly. The co-authors she selected in this book was done with intentionality. They will share real life stories that will not only inspire you but will also challenge you to leave your comfort zone. We ALL need leadership lessons from the trenches that will catapult us to the next level.

As I look over my life, I wish this book had been written when I was a teenager so I could have possibly avoided some of the pitfalls I experienced, identified what leadership looks like, and to provide me with tips to prepare me for an uncertain future. I am so happy that I have lived to see 43 years of life. I have seen the good, the bad, and the ugly. I nearly took my life when I was 38 years old. I was once a severe alcoholic who almost allowed my addiction to destroy me and everyone around me. But God! Although I hurt others as a result of the hurt I experienced, I'm living proof, like the ladies in this book ... that healing, and delivery are possible. I don't look like what I've been through. My achievements and accomplishments speak for themselves. With therapy, self-love and a change in perspective, I've overcome insurmountable odds and have become the leader I am today despite what others thought or said. I was removed from social media six years ago and NOW I am back better and stronger than ever.

Now, it's your turn to get out of your own way and accept that you also were born to lead. Are you ready? The world is waiting for you! You are your ancestor's wildest dreams to come true. Our future leaders, the next generation, are looking to you to lead the way.

"You don't become what you want, you become what you believe."
~ Oprah Winfrey

INTRODUCTION: IN THE BEGINNING A LEADER WAS BORN

JACQUELINE KABA-HARRISON

Do you believe you were born to lead? If so, then this book is for you! In addition to sharing my own leadership journey, *Born to Lead* includes the stories of seven powerful African American women who demonstrate diverse leadership styles on many levels. At some point throughout their life's experiences, they recognized that they possessed an innate ability to lead and lead well. As you read each chapter, their stories may resonate with you. May their testimonies of resiliency, adaptability, and strength cause you to recognize and embrace the leader within you. However, don't allow it to become dormant, it must be cultivated and applied in your personal and professional lives.

Often times, African American women are viewed as bossy, assertive, opinionated, and even aggressive. Perhaps you can relate and have been mislabeled as such in the workplace, at home, or even in your community, when in reality you were demonstrating leadership? Like you, the authors who contributed to this anthology are often the go-to persons for their bosses, immediate family members, church members, friends, and others. We make leadership look so easy at times because it comes naturally, yet, we aren't given the credit we deserve. However, when our skills go unnoticed and unacknowledged, oftentimes we lose out on promotion and other opportunities that will take us to the next level in our careers. In addition, it's not a secret that women are highly underpaid at disproportionate levels in comparison to their male counterparts.

But don't lose heart, allow the co-authors in this collaboration to inspire and encourage you in ways unimaginable. Continue to surround yourself with like-minded women who desire to lead by example because those coming behind you are watching and need you to guide them along the way.

Also, take a moment to reflect on the invaluable contributions of the following historical African American women and game changers who have led by example, including, but not limited to: Madam C.J. Walker, Harriet Tubman, Angela Davis, Zora Neale Hurston, Susie King Taylor, Clarissa M. Thompson, Phyllis Wheatley, Nannie Helen Burroughs, Constance Baker Motley, Mary Church Terrell, Mary McLeod Bethune, Clarissa Thompson, Laura A. Moore Westbrook, Katherine Johnson, Ida B. Wells, Hallie Quinn Brown, Frances E.W. Harper, Fannie Lou Hamer, Shirley Chisholm, Barbara Jordan, Fannie Barrier Williams, Patricia Harrison's as well as countless others who dedicated their lives as a result of their leadership to help make the United States a better place to live not only for African Americans, but for all. Imagine the amount of courage, dedication, and resiliency it must have taken for them to achieve what they did given the times they were living in? However, quitting was not an option and they persevered regardless of the challenges they faced.

About 10 years ago, I saw leadership with fresh eyes. I began to take notice how women in my family as well as others were holding down their households, careers, while making invaluable contributions to their communities. It was worth taking note of how they juggled numerous balls, but rarely dropped any. When adversity reared its ugly head, they didn't ask why me or felt victimized. To the contrary they held their head up high, made the best decisions they could and did the most with what they had. So when you hear the phrase "Black Girl Magic" it's real and continues to happen all around us every day. African American women all over the world are earning advanced degrees, managing Fortune 500 companies, earning six figures or more as business owners, and are traveling the world leaving their indelible mark on society. In other words, they're MAKING BOSS MOVES!

As I thought about my own journey, I would not have been successful if I hadn't developed an unshakable self-confidence. As a result, it has laid the very foundation on which I continue to build on while cultivating my leadership skills today. Although we may encounter hardships in life that may hinder us from developing this much-needed skill, don't be discouraged. Always remember that we stand on the shoulders of amazing trailblazers who have paved the way for us to be successful and unstoppable. Our time is now! Embrace the leader within and fly high. The best is yet to come.

"Success is liking yourself, liking what you do, and liking how you do it."
~ Maya Angelou

I AM LEADERSHIP
JACQUELINE KABA-HARRISON

Wow, I can't believe I am the visionary author of this book collaboration with seven other powerful women who are model leaders and have a desire to show others how to become the same. If someone would have asked me 15 years ago if I would be a part of a book collaboration on leadership I would have said, "Absolutely not." But here I am, along with seven other like-minded phenomenal women sharing my story about how I became the leader I am today.

"You are not that smart and will have to work two-to-three times harder than others to achieve the same thing." Although those words were spoken to me by my father when I was a child, I still hear them so vividly as if he said it yesterday and they still sting. Sometimes I become teary eyed when recalling this. I didn't feel worthy of abundance and didn't believe I deserved to be happy. I surely didn't believe I was smart enough to start my own business one day. My self-esteem was shattered, and I didn't trust my judgement to make sound decisions. There was a time when I didn't believe I had a story to tell. I didn't believe I had anything of value to share with anyone, much less something that would help other women. The bottom line is during that season of my life, I didn't value myself as a person, let alone a leader capable of pouring into others.

Fast forward to 2022, not only do I have a voice, but I also now know that I have a message that will help other women excel in life and build a better future for themselves and their families. I am excited about my journey and what the future holds. TODAY I BELIEVE IN ME!

It's a known fact that African American women have been a force throughout history from the Dynasties of ancient Egypt to the Civil Rights Movement during the 1960's. As African American women we have innate leadership abilities, and my hope is that those of you reading this book will accept your leadership crown and wear it proudly. Stop leading from behind the scenes in order to make others feel comfortable. Don't become intimidated when others call you bossy, aggressive, or arrogant ... all of the terms often used to portray Black women in a negative light. Rather, consider them as terms of respect, acknowledgement, and as compliments. Your leadership skills were given to you for a reason. DO NOT WASTE THEM!

When I think of leadership, this phenomenal Black woman comes to mind, is someone I truly admire, and she inspires me. Madam C. J. Walker was a smart businesswoman and a remarkable leader. She became successful during a time when typically only White men were allowed to do so. Despite her opposition, she believed in her ability to reach her goals and conquered them despite what anyone else thought. She's a credible example and a reminder to fellow African American women of how powerful, determined, resourceful and innovative we are. She has paved the way and laid a foundation for women of color to build on and who aspire to be business owners and entrepreneurs.

She is a woman after my own heart and because of her determination, I saw myself in her and is one of the reasons I decided to write Born to Lead.

There are many qualities and characteristics of a good leader. One quality is the ability to make sound decisions. As a leader, others will look to you for guidance, direction, effective decision making and able to solve problems. There was a time when I wasn't confident in my ability to make sound decisions without talking it over with at least two other people. I took a bold step outside of my comfort zone and started attending West African dance classes. Although I had danced my entire life this style of dancing was like nothing I had ever experienced before. It was like learning a new language. But I kept going back to class and over a period of time it had become a part of me. It boosted my confidence and was able to reverse the stigma that had plagued me many years of my life. I started believing that I could handle whatever came my way. Whenever I found myself in "unchartered waters," I no longer ran from it or doubted myself any longer. Rather, I would say, "I got this." Being confident is an essential quality for a leader to have.

Another essential leadership trait is adaptability, the ability to adjust to new and/or unexpected circumstances. Previously, I had difficulty in this area when it came to new experiences. I would become extremely anxious and feared the unknown. However, I eventually learned to face my fears head on given that change is inevitable. How I chose to respond to the situation determined the outcome. In most cases, I realized that I was making a mountain out of a molehill. Personally and professionally, life happens and often times it's unpredictable. That's when flexibility comes into play. No matter how much you plan ahead, the outcome may turn out differently. A good leader is able to think on his or her feet and make the necessary course corrections and move forward.

Another fundamental characteristic of a remarkable leader is resiliency ... the ability to recover quickly from disappointments, failure, difficulties, and/or obstacles. Growing up, if I failed at something it was a tremendous blow to my self-esteem and self-confidence. Depending on what it was it would hit me in my core leaving me feeling devastated and defeated. I would waste so much time beating myself up versus acknowledging what I could have done differently to achieve my desired result. It's all about perspective and the lens we choose to look through. I learned over time that my failures do not define me or change who I am at my core. Failure is a permitted response and is not common among strong leaders. Sometimes we have to get out of our own way and let nothing or no one get in the way of achieving our goals.

If life's experiences don't challenge you, they won't change you. There will be times when you'll want to give up and throw in the towel, but you must stay the course and deal with them. Avoiding the issue won't help either and isn't the mark of a strong leader. When you do this you are less likely to take risks and without taking risks there are no rewards. If you quit when things get hard you will decrease your chances of succeeding at anything. You will be less likely to reap the fruits from your hard work if you quit when the going gets rough. Remember that someone is always watching and needs to see leadership modeled in such a way that they will want to emulate the behavior. A resilient leader does not allow failure to cause them to doubt their ability to lead. Challenges present opportunities to learn and grow. Lessons reveal what worked well and what did not. However, it's only the lesson that's not learned from that's often repeated. As eloquently stated by the beautiful Lupita Nyong'o, "It's only when you risk failure that you discover things. When you play it safe, you're not expressing the utmost of your human experience."

Two additional qualities of a successful leader are authenticity and awareness. I am a firm believer that what separates great leaders from those who aren't is the ability to be authentic and self-aware. Self-awareness is important because you're able to identify your strengths as well as the areas that need work. Effective women leaders must be true to self, refrain from comparing themselves to others, and hold themselves accountable. Especially in the areas of coaching or mentoring, never be afraid of using yourself as an object lesson for those in your sphere of influence. Not only are you seen as credible, but you also create a safe space for others to be the same. There's nothing wrong with admiring other female leaders, but refrain from imitating them, thus diminishing your own uniqueness. You will never be as successful as you intend to be by mimicking others. Don't fall into the trap of suppressing your authenticity.

Last but not least all good leaders must possess self-confidence, which is defined as complete trust in one's abilities, qualities, and judgement to achieve a particular goal. Leaders with a strong self-confidence lead by example and are selfless. As a result, their subordinates find them believable and don't have a problem supporting them. To the contrary, if their ability to lead is questionable, those who report to them will reject their guidance. Would you allow yourself to be lead or influenced by someone who doesn't believe in themselves? Others will not align themselves with you if they sense self-doubt or a lack of ability to lead them.

The qualities and characteristics previously mentioned are what I embody day to day in my role as an entrepreneurial leader. But my journey has not been one void of challenges and obstacles. Many times I have had to and continue to step out on faith, operate outside of my comfort zone, celebrate my victories (big and small), practice mindful self-care, surround myself with like-minded individuals, extend forgiveness to myself and others, and eliminate self-sabotaging behaviors.

In the words of media mogul Oprah Winfrey, "You don't become what you want, you become what you believe." That said, so Queens stop hiding backstage, stop diminishing your accomplishments, stop downplaying your talents, stop doubting yourself, and stop dimming your light so others can shine! You come from a lineage of strong women leaders. So stand up and straighten your leadership crown!

BIOGRAPHY

Jacqueline Kaba-Harrison is a Confidence and Success Coach and the CEO of Realizing Your Potential LLC to empower and inspire African American women everywhere to maximize their potential and be the best version of themselves. Moreover, she helps other coaches and consultants create effective strategies to eliminate negative self-talk and self-sabotaging behaviors that prevent them from taking their business to the next level.

As an empowerment speaker, Jacqueline teaches entrepreneurs how to stay motivated, create an unshakeable confidence, and how to increase productivity in their businesses. She also helps them develop effective mindset strategies for success.

Additionally, she provides a virtual platform for entrepreneurs to receive personal, professional, and leadership development that's designed to help them grow their business. She is the Executive Producer of the "Queen's Round Table" Channel on the Women Win TV Network, the fastest growing all women network offered via the streaming service Roku as well as Amazon Fire TV. Jacqueline also serves as host of "A Queen's Round Table Leadership Symposium, television show and podcast. She is the visionary author of the *Born To Lead: Awakening the Leader Within Anthology* book project that includes the stories of seven additional women who have overcome hardships in their lives and managed not only to survive but thrive as leaders within their respective fields by acknowledging their innate strength, resiliency, adaptability and leadership qualities as African American women.

"I'm no longer accepting the things I cannot change … I'm changing the things I cannot accept."
~ Angela Davis

WHAT THE ENEMY MEANT FOR EVIL, GOD TURNED IT FOR MY GOOD

EBONY BUTLER

"Happy birthday to you! Happy birthday to you! Happy birthday to you, happy birthday to you!" That's the song my mom heard right before being rushed into the Labor and Delivery unit at the county hospital in Dallas, TX. How coincidental it was for me to be born on her 20th birthday? I was born in the town of Dallas, Oak Cliff in June of 1978 to two teenagers who started out as friends, and by me being born, I'm sure you know how that ended. My mom had recently withdrawn from Prairie View A & M University and my father had just returned home from serving a short stint in the United States Army. Back then there were only two socioeconomic classes for Black Americans -- middle-class or poor and I experienced both sides of the coin. My father was raised in a nice home with both parents and my mom was raised in the low-income apartments across the street by a single mom of six children. Born to parents with different upbringings truly has shaped me into who I am today.

Early on, I felt safe, secure, and loved by my parents, but also favored by my extended family of aunts, uncles and grandparents. I loved my family dearly and took pride in being connected to one of my aunts, because she was highly educated and defeated the odds. She was a radical for social justice and a graduate from Ohio State, and that was very uncommon back in the 80s. Because of her, I took a liking to one of the most zealous and courageous political activists and leaders during the Civil Rights movement – Angela Davis. The starvation for equality, justice, peace, and education was the common thread they both shared; and as I experienced my life's journey, I realized how important each of these factors were and how they played out over my life. Recognizing my strength and power materialized when I mentally connected with the struggles these ladies endured and how they overcame them with little to no resources during that time. Radically leading movements of thousands of people with persecution and hatred looming over your head is no easy feat; yet it can be done.

I was spoiled by my father's parents; yet, disciplined by my maternal grandmother, so as you can imagine, I became skilled in figuring out how to get my way. I was a happy child, always outside playing with my cousins, and pretending to be the teacher as we played school sitting on the staircase of our apartment complex, until the summer of 1982. I became very ill during that time and recall feeling feverish and weak very often. I seemed to get weaker each moment I laid in bed instead of going out to play. My mom would wake me through the night to clean me as I couldn't hold my bowels at all by this time. As a little kid, I'd apologize to her, and she would respond with, "It's ok baby, Momma will take care of you." While she assured me everything was going to be fine, I believe deep down she knew something was wrong. For months, my parents took me in and out of hospital emergency rooms and no one could tell them what was going on. This unknown sickness started to take a toll on my little body and I began to miss a lot of days from my pre-K class. After another bad and restless night my mom rushed me to the local hospital's children's unit. My parents felt defeated, discouraged, and helpless and would have never imagined that an older, white, gray-haired man who resembled Abraham Lincoln, would diagnose me with Graves' disease, an autoimmune disorder that causes the thyroid gland to make too much of the thyroid hormone. This disease is also known as hyperthyroidism. The excess thyroid hormone in my bloodstream caused my little body's metabolism to be too active which resulted in weight loss, brittle skin, bulging and dark eyes, a racing heart, and tiredness. At the age of four I was prescribed medicine that I had to take twice a day to treat this lifelong condition. It affects people differently, and as a child, one of the areas affected is one's school performance, so it's recommended for parents to work with school staff to alter learning plans to make learning easier.

Let me introduce myself, I am Ebony Butler and I graduated from high school as a student of the advanced graduate program.

My parents lived together until I was five after deciding to part ways and that's when my mom and I returned to live with my grandmother. She was a cashier at a restaurant; and she knew that wasn't enough to make ends meet. So every Sunday she'd get the newspaper and spread it out over our bed to circle places she'd contact to find work. There were times I could tell she was sad, and I would say to her, "Mommy, everything will be ok." I would wipe her tears as she hugged and played with me the rest of the day. I will never forget the day she received a call that changed the trajectory of our lives. Her application was received by a well-known technology company, who wanted to interview her for a position that she had no previous experience. Now that was favor! She got the job and we moved to the suburbs.

I know my mom thought this was best; yet, at the time, I was scared and often felt alone, and I was alone. This was my first-time experiencing unacceptance. I was enrolled at a predominately white school and the only Black student in my class. At the age of seven, I struggled with not being accepted by my peers in my new neighborhood, and on top of that, I also struggled when I went back to my hometown because I was teased for being a "sellout." Of course, at that age, I had no clue what a "sellout" was; however, I quickly learned – it was not a good thing.

Let me introduce myself, I am Ebony Butler, and I am a strategic partner focused on diversity, equity, and inclusion.

The first nine years of my life, it was me and my mom; and as a matter of fact, I almost feel as if my dad faded in the background after the passing of his mom, my dear grandmother. Although my dad's heart was broken, emotionally, I grew closer and closer to my mom. I was so proud of her. She was such a great mother and a hard worker and believe it or not, even at the age of nine, I appreciated and admired her. After years of just she and I, my baby brother was born. While some children grow envious or jealous towards their younger siblings, I did not. I loved my little brother and immediately dived into my role as a big sister. At age 13, my baby sister was born on my dad's side, and once again, I was so proud to be an older sister. I was raised during the "latchkey" generation and if you don't know, we were called "latchkey kids" because we would get out of school and go home to no adult supervision until our parents returned from work. My mom was always looking for a babysitter, even though I always tried to show her I was responsible enough to care for myself and my brother. Eventually she gave in and trusted me to stay home alone and care for my little brother. I wanted to step in and help her and I did it with ease. I taught, disciplined, played with, fed, and bathed my brother to make things easier for my mom and she was grateful, until I wound up pregnant at 16, my junior year in high school. Naturally, she was disappointed, and felt guilty because of the amount of responsibility I had been given at such an early age. . I was scared and angry with my mom at the time as I aborted my first unborn child.

However, I began to set my sights back on higher learning and aspired to attend Clark Atlanta University, majoring in education. I was determined to become an Algebra teacher. However, I continued my relationship with my boyfriend, and six months after aborting our first child, I was pregnant again. I was happy and viewed my pregnancy as retaliation and rebellion against my mom. I immediately told her I was pregnant again, and again; she was heartbroken. My mom has always been my biggest fan, but looking back, if we all admitted it, we felt hopeless about my future. I graduated from high school and shortly after, gave birth to my first child, a son Less than two years later, I gave birth to my daughter, so focusing on college was a distant thought, and working to provide for my children became my top priority. I was working hard to make ends meet while my children's father, the person who was my high school sweetheart, quickly turned into my high school nightmare. Sadly, he ran the streets day and night in my car and did not contribute much to the betterment of our family. Unfortunately, during our young relationship, abuse reared its ugly head in the form of mental, emotional, and physical abuse. My best friends tried to talk to me; but I chose to prove my mom and others wrong by staying and putting up with the fighting and arguing, just to keep my young family together. But hiding bruises and trying to escape to call 911 became a norm for me by this time. Early mornings I stood at the bus stop at

5:30 am, six months pregnant with my last child and holding the hands of the older two. Yes, by age 23, I had given birth to three children and their father was incarcerated. Although I was upset; I later thanked God for forcing me to accept a new path of life, just me and my three children.

Let me introduce myself, I am Ebony Butler, and I was a single mom of three children by age 23.

The last few years of my abusive relationship, I was always told that I'd never amount to anything, and no one would ever desire me having three children at such a young age. I heard this over and over from more people than I can count, and it was disheartening. However, I threw myself into caring for my children and working hard to afford a better life for us all. During that time, I met a man who countered everything I had been told and fell head over heels and ladies, you know exactly what I mean. After two years of dating we were married and soon after that, we bought our first home. I finally felt accomplished and complete. I was a mother, a wife, a homeowner, and just like my mom – a hard worker. At this point of my life, I was full of excitement, and I felt optimistic about our future. As a matter of fact, I started college and received my bachelor's degree in business management. While I was moving closer towards accomplishing my own personal dreams, unfortunately my marriage was falling apart, and my dear father's days were nearing to an end. I had no idea things would take a dramatic turn for the worse. Unexpectedly, my father passed away from an aneurysm. I beat myself up because I failed to go see him during Christmas, because as quiet as it was kept, I was somewhat angry with him. Although I felt his love as a child; as I grew into a young woman, I didn't feel he protected me much. While mourning the loss of my dad, my husband and I were arguing daily about our finances, the children, and the random and mysterious phone calls that started happening in the middle of the night. Unfortunately, adultery consumed my husband, our marriage ended, and it left me hurt, insecure, heartbroken, confused, disappointed, guilty, hopeless, and most of all, angry, broke, and a few months away from homelessness. My husband did not have kids of his own and his family felt I was looking for gold when I met him because I came into the marriage with three children. I couldn't believe this was happening and at the time, I was hoping it was a bad dream because I wanted my marriage to work. I wanted to defeat the odds and keep this blended family together; and I failed.

Let me introduce myself, I am Ebony Butler, a divorcee, fatherless, and single again with three children by age 33.

The house I was so excited to get was now up for foreclosure. Vehicles I purchased had past due payments and my credit and bank accounts were a mess. I frequently got payday loans that I refinanced so many times I paid the initial loan amount two to three times over. In spite of everything, I was able to muster up the money to find my children and I another house to live in. I cried at nights reflecting on everything that was said to me throughout the years; especially after having kids so young; and I started to feel that everything I had heard was right. I wasn't going to be anything. I was an embarrassment. No one in their right mind would ever love me. I spiraled into days and days of depression, and I was no good to anyone – not even my children. Physically, I was there, yet; emotionally and mentally I was distant. I was struggling to make ends meet. I prayed to get home from work on the gas fumes left in my vehicle. I would pray and cry at work so much, I had to eventually take a leave of absence because I no longer focused on anything, and my work began to suffer. Things progressively got worse and by this point, money was so tight, I decided to get a second job. Through it all, my children never knew there were nights I would force myself to sleep while hungry; and how pleased I was that I could make them dinner, but it just wasn't enough for all of us. During these times, I learned humility, compassion, and strength. I felt like the woman described in the following quote by Eleanor Roosevelt, "A woman is like a tea bag; you never know how strong she is until she gets into hot water." This resonated with me so deeply and it encouraged me to pull myself out of the trenches of depression, brokenness, sadness, fear, disempowerment, and penuriousness! I also drew strength from the following words of Angela Davis, "The process of empowerment cannot be simplistically defined in accordance with our own particular class interests. We must learn to lift as we climb." These words inspired me to take control of my destiny and to walk boldly into my purpose, lifting others as I climbed!

Let me introduce myself, I am Ebony Butler, and my strength was realized through my struggle.

I continued working two jobs until I applied for a position at work that truly changed my life. With a promotion, I was still underpaid and had to work up the courage to speak with my boss about increasing my salary. Although I loved it and was really good in this role, I was contemplating leaving the job if my request would be denied. I wasn't totally convinced that after speaking with him things would change because I had never heard of someone asking for more money – except when negotiating a salary upon taking a role – and actually getting what they asked. However, my boss asked me to give him time to see what he could do because he understood my worth and contribution to the company. So I waited. Three weeks later, I received a call from the business owner offering me more than what I asked for. I accepted and my pay was increased that day. My increased salary was truly a life changer, and I thanked her every time I saw her for making the decision and listening to my boss. I also thanked him for believing in me and working diligently to increase my pay given that he knew what I had been up against personally. Life started to flow smoother for me and my family. I was promoted again to a position that required me to travel and work primarily from home. Not only did this position allow me to see the world and gain different experiences, but it also allowed me to be hands on with my kids when I was working from home. My son graduated and joined the United States Navy, and I welcomed my mom into my home to help me take care of the younger two as I traveled week to week. I also enrolled in a graduate program and received my MBA. What a perfect situation! All was well; however I didn't know that things were about to manifest in ways that would pose more problems for my family.

Let me introduce myself, I am Ebony Butler and people are beginning to believe in me.

My daughter went off to school, two years after my oldest son joined the Navy. Now that the older two were gone pursuing their passions, I was a stone throw away from being an empty nester because my youngest and last child was left to graduate. After my divorce, my credit was damaged and my bank account was drained; but, after four years of being on my own, I improved my creditworthiness and financial status, and did something I was afraid to do. I purchased my own home – building it from the ground up! I picked out the floor plan, the cabinets, floors ... I mean everything! I was the first one to live in this home and I was pleased because I did it all on my own! As the children began moving out on their own, my mom was becoming extremely attached to and dependent on me for her emotional and financial needs. The closeness we had when I was a young child was even more intense now; yet our roles flip flopped – or at least that's how it appeared to me. My mom had fallen on hard times over the years; so, when I took her in initially, I thought everyone would benefit; but circumstances became intolerable. I often felt like she and my children were competing for my time and attention, and this added a level of stress on me that was unbearable at times. She drowned in her problems and pain instead of facing them head on and my youngest son began to demonstrate behaviors that were unacceptable at home and at school. The closeness I once had with him, was now nonexistent. He began doing things that were totally uncharacteristic of the person I raised and once knew. My home lacked peace. I began to disconnect and withdraw from everyone again. A few run-ins with the law landed my son in juvenile detention. What's so unusual is that my employer knew none of this was going on. My boss would be shocked to learn that I was traveling the world teaching, speaking and inspiring others; and all the while, I had no idea where my son was the night before.

I learned that it was taboo for women of color, particularly Black women to unearth their true selves let alone bring their authentic selves to the corporate work place, so I kept silent. Exercising wisdom, I never shared anything I was going through at work to prevent it from negatively impacting my career or personal brand. Surprisingly, my son graduated high school; but, with no plans for his future. As his mom, that was hurtful, but I still stood by his side, until the third time he went to jail, and I was done. I had to regain my peace and happiness and I knew I couldn't do that by continuing to support and run to the aid of a person who clearly didn't want the best for his life. I learned to "no longer accept things I couldn't change; and to change the things I couldn't accept," quoted by Davis. So I began to read more, learn new skills, pray and meditate on scripture to clear my head, my heart, and my life. I focused on self-care, healing and truly just loving me. I know we are told to never be selfish, and I counter that; because in order to regain my power, I had to be selfish and get to know myself, independently of the title of mom, daughter, business professional, and companion. I had to get to know and love ME. I also started teaching at a historically black college and university. I accomplished my dream of becoming an educator, even though I wasn't teaching Algebra.

Every day I get up feeling blessed to be able to do what God told me I'd do. I reflect on the little whisper I heard when I was five years old, sitting on the steps of the apartment complex pretending to teach my cousins and friends, "You will speak and teach one day, and people will listen." I know that was from God and ever since, I've done just that.

Let me reintroduce myself. My name is Ebony Butler.

As a teen mom, I experienced many adversities, trials and tribulations. I have lost loved ones along the way in death, and in their mental ineptness to connect with me. I have been talked about, doubted, and wronged and guess what, I've wronged others too. I did not go to a traditional university, and I still made it. Now I'm a professor, speaker, teacher, consultant, coach, and an author! I chose to learn from all of my hardships and to be thankful for them. My setbacks set me up for career success. I now understand the quote by Angela Davis, "Walls turned sideways are bridges." What is meant to separate us from our purpose, pose as a barrier to keep us controlled, and what's meant to keep us from seeing the other side serves as a connection to our purpose in life. I've learned we have to shift how we think about circumstances in life in order to defeat any and every obstacle that comes our way. Humility, persistence, assertiveness, patience, and optimism were developed through my hard times and have added value to how I lead, consult, and grow others today. When I work with leaders, I lead with an equitable mindset. I truly agree with Ms. Davis when she says, "I have a hard time accepting diversity as a synonym for justice. Diversity is a corporate strategy."

BIOGRAPHY

Ebony Butler is a teacher, speaker, and consultant who knew early on she was blessed with the gift to speak, so she guards and protects that skill in everything she does. She is also the mother of three adult children. She was born, raised and currently resides in Dallas, Texas. She was an only child for nine years before her brother was born. Being a big sister has always been an important role for her and is one she credits for shaping her into the woman she is today, along with being raised by an independent and hardworking single mom.

Professionally, Ebony partners with leaders to help them refocus, rethink and reimagine how they approach their workforce today to welcome in women and people of color. She also enjoys her role as an adjunct professor at a historically black college and university where she is able to stay connected to the younger generations of people who will eventually become leaders. Ebony is most fulfilled when she's collaborating with organizations focused on supporting underserved communities by upskilling the youth, teen moms, and young women as they enter and navigate the workforce.

"There's power in allowing yourself to be known and heard,
in owning your unique story,
in using your authentic voice."
~Michelle Obama

QUEEN, ADJUST YOUR CROWN AND LEAD

DR. NAKITA DAVIS

Your voice, your message, your essence in the atmosphere is not only warranted and wanted, but it's needed. I learned the power of my voice in elementary school. I sang in chorus, was on the school news team as lead anchor, and often found myself taking up for the new kid or quiet girl in school.

What I didn't know was that God was preparing me to be a voice for the voiceless and a leader in my own right. As we grow into adults, we often don't realize that we have the power to lead right where we are!

I am the proud Chief Executive Officer and Founder of Jesus, Coffee, and Prayer Christian Publishing House LLC., and the Women Win Network, where we celebrate women who win 365 days a year, seven days a week. For years now, I've been immensely blessed to help women of all ages discover their voice and strengthen their passion and purpose, all while making an impact and a profit.

To Whom Much is Given, Much is Required

When we think about all of the commitments on our to-do list, the requirement can feel like a burden sometimes. But always remember – your voice and your mission matters.

When I think about all of the amazing women, who I affectionately refer to as Queens, who have come before me, my heart is filled with gratitude and Godly adoration. They have kicked down doors, crushed glass ceilings, and have defied boundaries, so you and me could be positioned to SOAR.

A Seat at the Table
When we choose to use our voice to enlighten, inspire, encourage, empower, challenge the status quo, and elevate other women who look just like us, we make our table long, wide, and inviting with endless possibilities. Now more than ever, it takes an authentic leader – one with a servant's attitude and bathed in humility, but as fierce as a lioness, to enable others to WIN.

Reflection
I was often called by my peers to right the wrongs both in school and while working in the corporate sector for almost 15 years. I often addressed the inconsistencies of senior management that made personnel feel powerless, overworked, or muted. I often felt like the little "Dr. Martin Luther King, Jr." of my peer groups, because I always found myself speaking up, and negotiating on behalf of those who couldn't quite articulate the words that needed to be said.

Your Voice Matters
An effective leader can be characterized by many traits and it's not always the person who barks the loudest in the room. Rather, a true leader in my book can be identified by having the following five invaluable traits:

Faith — In order to lead others, you must have faith. You must know that God will do what He said He will do. Also, you have to believe in yourself, the bigger picture, the end result, and the company you keep. If you take on a mission, but have no faith, then you are setting yourself and your team up to fail. Having faith does not always mean the absence of fear in a particular situation, as we are all human and have emotions. But it does mean that your faith trumps your fear. You move forward despite what you can see and despite your current situation.

Understanding — If you want to rally the troops, your team, and your supporters in business and in life, you must be willing to lean in and understand the very people you're serving. Do your research and effectively listen to the needs, the pain points, the fears, and the wants to gain clarity about their strengths. Only a fool jumps in the water without making a full assessment of their circumstances. When you gain adequate understanding about those you're leading, it shows them that you care. The old saying is, "People need to know that you care before they care to know what you know." Effective communication is key to understanding.

Integrity — Sadly, in both ministry and in the marketplace, this has been a growing issue with many leaders. *Merriam-Webster* defines integrity as follows:

1: firm adherence to a code of especially moral or artistic values : INCORRUPTIBILITY

2: an unimpaired condition: SOUNDNESS

3: the quality or state of being complete or undivided: COMPLETENESS

I like to break it down into these simplified terms – do what you say you are going to do, and when you can't, or when you fall short, humble yourself, take ownership, and communicate with your stakeholders honestly. Do the right thing even when no one is looking.

This sounds simple enough, but many fall short in this area. Leading with integrity does NOT mean perfection. None of us are perfect. But we can serve from a perfect place of love and willingness to get the job done. Often pride gets in the way of good leaders becoming GREAT when they don't want to admit they are wrong, have fallen short, or missed the mark.

As an effective leader, give yourself grace when mistakes are made; but hold yourself accountable to always do the right thing. Doing this will earn and keep the respect of your tribe and those who you serve. Not doing this overtime will spread like a cancer and kill the promise and purpose over your life. It is that critical.

Inspiration — How can you lead if no one is willing to follow? Effective leaders must boldly and authentically inspire others to be greater, to maximize their full potential, to see themselves in a brighter and better light, and capable of achieving the impossible. After all, impossible really translates as "I'm-possible!" The pivotal key here is to not be gimmicky or try the latest fad of some alleged guru, but to be yourself. People know when you are not being your authentic self.

It is a smack in God's face and a waste of time for you to be ANYTHING or ANYONE that He did not create you to be. Real people inspire real people. You'd be surprised who will glean from your poverty-stricken upbringing, past abusive relationship, drop-out-of-college story, or dead-end job to your successful entrepreneurial endeavor. People want to be inspired quite frankly; they need it. And you have just what it takes to give them hope for a better future with your voice, honest actions, and sound leadership.

Results Driven…But People Lead

You can have faith, understanding, be a woman of integrity, and inspire the world; but if you refuse to ACT with your heart and mind, all of your efforts will be in vain. "Faith without works is dead." ~ James 2:26

People may hear you; people may see you, but as an effective leader that is built to last, you always want to make people feel you! People feel the sincerity of your actions. Those who want you to win will position you to WIN in a real and tangible way. They will pick up the phone on your behalf, mention your name in rooms of influence and affluence, and do the work required to lead their team to victory. I speak these things because I live and breathe them by faith in Christ.

When I worked in the corporate arena before becoming a full-time CEO of two successful businesses, I formulated mentorship programs to help non-management employees thrive and transition into leadership and management positions. Many of my mentees have been promoted, as well as gained new experiences. All glory belongs to God, but that same skill set has now benefitted me and the women I serve worldwide.

Through various speaker platforms, books, and public relations campaigns that I've been fortunate enough to create, women around the world are stepping up to SOAR to higher heights, achieve the impossible, and break generational curses by becoming first-time international, best-selling authors, step on global stages, and reach the world with their voices. It's all because I said YES to my calling and my purpose. I'll say it again, your voice matters.

Being an effective leader does not mean having more followers, it's about creating and developing **MORE LEADERS**! This is the true jewel in your crown.

My hope is that these few tips on leadership will help you rethink, readjust your crown, and LEAD! I'm rooting for you to WIN BIG!

Queen, the time to take your royal position is NOW!

BIOGRAPHY

For a combined 25 times, **Dr. Nakita Davis** has been heralded as a best-selling author in the United States and internationally. Also to her credit, she's an award-winning publisher, a public relations guru, and global influencer. She is a Presidential Lifetime Achievement Award Winner, two-time Presidential Volunteer Service Award winner, as well as an AT&T Dream in Black honoree alongside Queen Latifah, P. Diddy Combs, and Rev. Al Sharpton.

She is the Chief Executive Officer of Jesus, Coffee, and Prayer Christian Publishing House LLC and the Women Win Network, helping thousands of women around the globe to live out their God-sized dreams of authorship and gained notoriety through her robust publishing and PR platform.

Dr. Davis has collaborated with best in class, including Eric Thomas, Les Brown, Trent Shelton, Dr. Sonja Stribling, Dr. Cheryl Wood, Bravo's "Married to Medicine" Dr. Heavenly Kimes, Grammy Award-winner Dorinda Clark-Cole, Jekalyn Carr, "Love & Marriage Huntsville's" Kimmi Grant, and more. Her campaigns have been featured at the Grammys, Super Bowl, Stellar Awards, and in Time Square in New York City. Dr. Davis's clients have been featured on MTV, BET, Blavity, all of the major television networks, in Sheen Magazine, as well as USA Today.

She is a proud member of For(bes) the culture, a platform of FORBES for elite professionals crushing glass ceilings and barriers for people of color.

Follow Dr. Nakita Davis on Instagram @ jesuscoffeeandprayer and @womenwinnetwork.

"It's only when you risk failure that you discover things. When you play it safe, you're not expressing the utmost of your human experience."
~Lupita Nyong'o

BELIEVE IN YOUR "LEADERSHIPRENEUR" ABILITIES

SONYA DAVIS

"Believe in yourself, learn, and never stop wanting to build a better world."

The words leader, educator, and entrepreneur (I affectionally call "leadershipreneur") all work together harmoniously. That said, having excellent "leadershipreneur" skills is one of the most prevalent attributes of a good educator and entrepreneur. An educator, philanthropist, womanist, and civil rights activist, Dr. Mary McLeod Bethune stated, "Believe in yourself, learn, and never stop wanting to build a better world." One lesson I have learned in life is to believe in myself and continue to learn. I consider myself a lifelong learner and believe there is a lesson learned in everything in life, albeit good and bad. For many decades, I have been both a proud educator and entrepreneur. Although I have had many challenges along the way, (i.e., surviving an abusive relationship, a bad accident, a job layoff, and divorce), each leadership role was rewarding and equipped me to help build a better world for me and my family.

"For I am my mother's daughter."

My mother was the first leader in my life. She was one of the first in her family to attend college and became pregnant with me when she was 19 years old. She wanted a better life for me and decided to allow my maternal grandparents to raise me until she was financially stable enough to provide for me.

My maternal grandparents were part of the great migration – a time between 1916 and 1970 when African Americans moved from the south to the north for better opportunities. In the 1960s, my grandfather secured a job with Ford Motor Company in Detroit, Michigan. He and my grandmother were proud homeowners of a modest home on the westside of "The Motor City." I learned many leadership skills and started a few job hustles as a young child. My biggest cheerleaders were my grandparents and my mother. Like Dr. Bethune, who began working in the fields at five years old, I had a small business braiding hair on my grandmother's porch and a lemonade stand at six years old. I essentially was born to lead by example, by watching my mother and grandparents work ethic. At 19, my mother began a long successful career with BellSouth in Atlanta, Georgia (now known as AT&T) and retired early in management at the age of 49! My grandfather also retired early from a management role at Ford Motor Company. Although they worked hard in leadership roles for many years, they were able to retire and travel. What good is a leader without enjoying the benefits of leadership?

"Greatness is largely a social accident, and almost always socially supported."

I believe that at some point in life, all people tend to experience greatness as leaders. However, some people are natural-born leaders, while others may gain a leadership role based on socioeconomic reasons related to a professional, academic, or personal shift. Perhaps the socioeconomic life shift may force a potential leader to become the leader they were meant to be. I was presented with a leadership role professionally and academically, however a personal shift threatened it.

Although I was active in high school, I did not serve or pursue leadership roles because I chose to begin working at the age of 16. I did enough to get by and was not motivated to pursue a leadership role. I did become homecoming queen during my senior year in high school, and some may consider representing my school in such a way to have been a form of leadership. I also decided not to attend college immediately after high school. However, I did enroll as a non-traditional undergraduate student, at age 35. I worked a part-time and full-time job, while attending college full-time. I was proud to graduate with a Bachelor of Science degree in Information Systems with honors. As a college student, I worked for a medical software development firm during the "dot.com era" when many online companies opened and closed. This was my first experience being laid off. One day, when I showed up to work, I could not enter the building because the doors were locked and had a sign that read, "This organization is closed. Please call us at this number for further information." My co-workers and I were in shock – not knowing what to do and where to go. I vowed to move into human resource management and develop a better way of handling a layoff than how my former employer handled our dismissal.

> **"Education is the great American adventure, the world's most colossal democratic experiment."**

After my layoff, I secured a position as an Assistant Human Resource Manager at a law firm. The leadership HR function that I loved the most was training and development. After my undergraduate graduation, I immediately pursued a Master of Science in Human Resource Management. Once I completed my graduate degree, I was promoted and became an HR Manager. In 2008, I enrolled in a doctoral education program at Southern Mississippi University.

Eventually, I transitioned from an HR Manager to a Training and Development Manager with a different law firm. After changing positions, I knew immediately that I had a true passion leadership! One attribute of a leader is passion. If a person is passionate about what they do, they most likely will do well. I love training people and watching them grow and learn new things, so I decided to pursue a position in the field of education and relocated to Louisiana. I landed my first leadership position in higher education at the University of Louisiana Monroe as the Assistant Director and Coordinator of Prior Learning Assessment and Online Learning. I also secured a part-time teaching job at Louisiana Delta Community College where I met my first mentor, Joseph Lane, the Program Director of the School of Business there. He taught business courses in the same building where I was assigned, and he and I became fast friends. He hired me as a part-time business instructor without prior experience. He said, "You have plenty of real-world business and leadership experience. Look around you – many things that we do are connected to business and leadership. Teach others what those things are to you."

To those of you with your years of service still ahead, the challenge is yours. Stop doubting yourselves. Have the courage to make up your minds and hold your decisions." Refuse to be BOUGHT for a nickel, or a million dollars, or a job!"

We often doubt ourselves as leaders or may have a "Disneyfication" perception of our leadership roles. For example, I doubted myself quite a bit as a leader and developed "imposter syndrome," which is defined as an internal experience of believing that you are not as competent as others perceive you to be. I questioned my knowledge, skills, and abilities for many years. I developed imposter syndrome while enrolled in the doctoral program at Southern Mississippi University. I naively compared myself to my classmates and professors and thought I was not smart enough. I was the only African American and felt out of place at first. After becoming friends with many of my classmates, I soon learned that they felt the same way I did. I learned not to compare myself with other people. Each of us has our own narrative, skills, and abilities.

"In each experience of my life, I have had to step out of one little space of the known light, into a large area of darkness. I had to stand awhile in the darkness and then gradually God has given me light. But not to linger in. For as soon as that light has felt familiar, then the call has always come to step out ahead again into new darkness."

On the evening of October 23rd, 2013, as I prepared for work, something felt off. It was a feeling of dread and anxiety. The following morning, it seemed as if everything was moving in slow motion. I could not sleep and woke up a few hours early. On my way to work, I was in deep thought as I planned my morning. It was still dark, and up ahead, I saw a caravan of tractor-trailers at a stop sign. One truck stopped at the stop sign and continued across the road, and the next truck did the same. However, the last truck did not stop, and the truck driver ran the stop sign. I looked over to the right in a state of horror as I witnessed this 18-wheeler heading toward my vehicle. I panicked and tried to turn the car, but the truck driver t-boned my vehicle. Sadly, I remember thinking this was how I was going to die. As my vehicle flipped continuously, I thought about my mother, friends, family, co-workers, and students who I would never see again.

After my vehicle's third or fourth flip, I lost consciousness and made peace by acknowledging I was dying and calling out to God for help. I told him how much I loved him and was ready to go. I do not know how much time passed by, but when I gained consciousness, my car was upside down, and there was glass and blood everywhere, and I smelled smoke. I screamed in shock, then realized I had to calm my nerves and get the hell out of the wreckage.

Two men ran over to help me, and I told them that I could not get out of the seat belt because it jammed. Eventually, they pulled me from the car, and I could hear an ambulance and police sirens approaching. I do not remember anything after this, but the police officer shared months later that I said, "I have an 8:00 class. Can someone call my supervisor because I will be late for work?" Despite the terrible accident, my work ethic shined through! I was airlifted to the hospital via helicopter, and although I was in immense pain and had severe Vertigo, I did not have one broken bone!

Remember the two men who saved my life? No one saw them. The EMT who took a picture of my car did not see them either, but their red truck is clearly in the picture. I know they were my guardian angels. To date, no one ever located them. I tried for years to find them but to no avail. I wanted to hug them both and thank them for saving me. My car caught fire minutes after they pulled me out. I will never forget their act of kindness and bravery.

Doctors explained that I might experience a lifetime of short-term memory loss due to having a concussion and other trauma from the accident. The emergency room doctor also explained that I would eventually need replacement knee surgery (to date, I have chronic knee pain from the accident). I also experienced panic attacks and anxiety whenever driving. I started seeing a therapist who helped me with the anxiety, panic attacks, and memory loss. He also informed me that the trauma I received from the accident wasn't the only trauma I was suffering from, but there was evidence of unresolved childhood trauma, as a result of abandonment issues from not having a father in my life. I was told that if I did not deal with my problems, my problems would continue to deal with me.

As a leader, it is essential to humbly embrace who we are and who we would like to be – flaws and all. For many years, I hid that I had issues with my memory from my family and friends. I was a subject matter expert on ??? whose livelihood depended on the knowledge I shared with others. How could I continue as an educator and doctoral student if my memory were compromised?

Because of my memory loss and anxiety issues, I felt inadequate and a shell of the person I once was. My family, friends, co-workers, and students thought I had it all together, yet I could not remember the most inconsequential day-to-day things – lesson plans, what someone told me a few minutes prior, reminders, and I constantly would lose things, my phone, my car keys, where I placed my mail, or lyrics to songs. I was depressed, sad, frustrated, and scared that I would continue to have memory loss for the rest of my life.

Before my car accident, I made $90K per year teaching online, in addition to my salary as a full-time college instructor. Unfortunately, because of my health challenges I had to resign from all of my online teaching jobs, and due to financial hardship, I had no choice but to file Chapter 7 bankruptcy, and I became homeless. I was sleeping in my vehicle and would arrive to work very early so I could wash up; but no one knew this. One of my co-workers Janet allowed me to stay with her during the week because I had to travel 85 miles to work one way from where I resided. My "tribe" – consisting of family, friends, and co-workers -- thought I stayed with Janet because I had anxiety while driving, and although this was true – I did not tell anyone about my homelessness.

There is a profound reason why I am sharing the "not so pretty" side of my life. When the makeup is gone, and the flaws are evident, despite everything I experienced, the leader mentality never left. Leaders are human. We smile and laugh, attend speaking engagements, all while managing and leading other people. We have great pictures and advice to post on social media and based on appearance, we seem to have it all together. But, whew chile, I was further from the truth – I was a whole, hot mess. I was in a continuous foggy, dark place. Life was heavy, and I did not see any positive relief, but I started to remember I was a warrior, and that God never left my side. He gave me another chance to live from my horrific accident and had more significant works in store for me, but it was up to me to formulate a plan of action and execute it!

> **"A woman is free if she lives by her own standards and creates her own destiny if she prizes her individuality and puts no boundaries on her hopes for tomorrow."**

Eventually, parts of my memory were restored, but there were still times that I didn't remember certain things, but with the help of various forms of therapy and brain exercises, I have persevered and managed well. I also started to take charge of my financial issues by learning strategies to manage my money well by saving more and increasing my credit score. As a result, I started saving my income. I also became frugal with spending money and shopping. Eventually, my credit score improved, my savings increased, and I made additional income by teaching extra courses and teaching during the summer.

In 2018, I got married, quit my job, and moved back to Atlanta, Georgia. I had enough savings for a year, and my husband's income was enough to cover our household expenses. Unfortunately, within a year, my marriage started failing. I was silently dealing with domestic abuse and began planning my escape. I decided to return to work and secured a teaching position with a technical college. I also started a real estate staging business.

Then the COVID-19 pandemic hit the United States, and within months, I dissolved my real estate staging business, and was laid off from my teaching position. Again, I did not have any income, and my husband's home improvement business failed. We started living off of credit cards, the money I saved was long gone, and I was in a panic, similar to everyone else. I was also trapped in a house with an domestic violence abuser during the lockdown phase of the pandemic. My only saving grace was my mother and cousin, who came to live with us. While they were living with us, my husband was not abusive and wore a mask in front of them. I also wore a mask because I had to hide the reality of my marriage from my family and friends.

When a person is in a position of drastic change, they can experience two types of mindsets – a growth mindset or a fixed mindset. A person with a fixed mindset thinks negatively, blames others, and does not develop a positive action plan. However, a person with a growth mindset develops a plan of action, has patience, and is optimistic about their future. I chose the latter and applied for unemployment, and professionally networked with previous colleagues, friends, and associates by joining Facebook and LinkedIn groups in my profession. I also reached out to previous places of employment and is why one should never burn bridges! You never know when you might have to cross them again. Secretly, I was still planning to leave my marriage, and I opened a secret bank account and a post office box to receive mail that I did not want my husband to see.

> **"Faith is the first factor in a life devoted to service. Without it, nothing is possible. With it, nothing is impossible."**

Months later, my unemployment was approved, and I received a two-month lump sum, as well as weekly unemployment benefits. With a positive mindset and great networking, I secured four online part-time teaching positions. One of them eventually became full-time! I am now happily divorced, still healing from the trauma of domestic abuse and my car accident. I am also branding a career coaching business based on my many years of human resource management experience and a passion for helping people to find remote teaching positions. I also developed a passion for writing and have participated in a few book anthologies, including this one! In addition, I am currently writing a book about networking and career strategies – soon to be released this year.

None of my success would be possible without my tribe and mentors. Their love never wavered, and they are consistently there to encourage me through my many facets of my life. However, I have an extended tribe consisting of a network of colleagues and people I have never met who have my best interest at heart.

"Invest in the human soul. Who knows, it might be a diamond in the rough."

Mentorship is a valuable leadership tool. Although there are various levels as an educator, I also embrace opportunities to mentor others continuously by sharing ideas, resources, and knowledge because I am passionate about helping others. I have also had the privilege of having quite a few mentors help me along the way – my maternal grandparents, my mother, my Uncle San, a father figure to me, my previous manager, Joe who gave me a chance to teach, and my previous supervisor, Kim, who was patient during the rehabilitation phase after my car accident, who continues to provide glowing recommendations and has helped me secure teaching positions. My current supervisor, Jenny, encourages me to be the best educator I can be and offers various opportunities for professional growth. She's someone I can call and genuinely laugh hysterically with or discuss what we are currently reading with one another.

I leave you love. I leave you hope. I leave you with the challenge of developing confidence in one another. I leave you a thirst for education. I leave you a respect for the use of power. I leave you with faith. I leave you racial dignity. I leave you a desire to live harmoniously with your fellow man. I leave you finally, with a responsibility to our young people."

I had to learn to meet people – where they are versus where I am in order to understand them, learn from them, or be unbothered by them. Everything in life is a lesson learned, including those from my encounters with every human being who I have had the privilege of meeting along my life journey, albeit good or bad, they have helped me build character and become a better leader who is evolving each day.

Remember that YOU matter, and everyone is a beginner at something and has to start from somewhere. I humbly appreciate how others helped me in the beginning, middle, and throughout my leadership journey. Although life's circumstances and people may disappoint me, I remind myself there are many valuable lessons to gain from each experience. People are who they are, and life is what it is. I choose to believe in God, embrace happiness when it shows up, and help as many people as I can along the way. The "leadershipreneur" in me will prevail with faith and perseverance!

Editor's note: *All quotes in bold are attributed to Dr. Mary McLeod Bethune.*

BIOGRAPHY

Sonya Davis, affectionately known as Coach Sonya, is a co-author, online college instructor, business owner, and a certified career coach. She is the founder of Coach Sonya Consulting, LLC and previously owned Atlanta Staging Creations, LLC, a real estate staging business, as well as a bookstore, Books & Beignets, LLC. She has 15 years of teaching experience and is not new to career coaching or the human resource management field.

Coach Sonya is a proud native of Atlanta, Georgia, and spent many childhood summers with her maternal grandparents in Detroit, Michigan. She currently splits her time between her home state and Arkansas. She earned a Bachelor of Science in Information Systems from Mercer University and a Master of Science in Human Resource Management from Troy University. Presently, she's enrolled in a doctoral program with a focus on business administration.

When she is not writing, coaching, or teaching remotely, Coach Sonya spends most of her downtime reading, walking, practicing yoga, traveling, and spending time with family and friends. An avid sports fan, you can find her cheering on her favorite teams, the Detroit Lions, Atlanta's Braves, Hawks, and Falcons, as well as the Georgia Bulldogs at many different sporting events.

"The most common way people give up their power is by thinking they don't have any."
~ Alice Walker

LEAD AND LEAVE YOUR MARK ON THE WORLD

ANGELA LEWIS

"A true leader has the confidence to stand alone, the courage to make tough decisions, and the compassion to listen to the needs of others." ~ **Douglas MacArthur**

When I first found out about this project, I was super excited because the title of the anthology resonated with my spirit. I've been in some form of a leadership role for as long as I can remember. Growing up, I was the eldest sibling in my household, eight years older than my sister and 10 years older than my brother. So, what appeared to be a bossy nature, was me tapping into the leadership skills I was born with.

Leadership came easily and naturally to me because of the examples I saw in my own home. My father was the pastor of a church, and my mother was the manager of a school cafeteria. It seemed like they were always listening to the needs of others and leading them to something better. It was inspiring to watch them talk to people and see the growth and transformation that came from their leadership influence.

Although leadership was a natural fit, it wasn't always something I chose to do. In fact, I feel like leadership chose me! I preferred to be in the background and allow someone else to take charge; however, people would look to me or volunteer me to be the go-to person. It wasn't that I didn't feel capable because I did. My problem was being a people-pleaser and wanting everyone to like me. It was bad enough that none of my friends were in the classes I took during school. I did not want my being the leader of something to be another reason that kept me from being included in the circle.

I struggled with assuming leadership positions well into adulthood. The funny thing is, I always had great ideas, and as soon as I said them, someone would say, "You should be the one to implement it and lead the team to accomplish the goal." Eventually, I accepted the inevitable. Although I tried to hide it, I was born to lead, and it was time to awaken the leader within!

I attended a church in 2007, content to sit on the pew, absorb the word and go home. Ironically, it all came back to the church. I joined the "Connection Team," which was made up of a team of ushers and greeters, but who were also assigned to the new members who joined the church. Initially, I just wanted to call and thank the visitors for attending and welcome the new members; however, that didn't last long. I was given the opportunity to become a part of the leadership team and run the New Members Department.

I absolutely loved what I did. The leader within was awakened, and I was in my element. My team was on fire, and we were operating like a well-oiled machine. We were getting the new members acclimated to the church and placed in ministries that matched their gifts and talents. We held monthly new member classes as well as quarterly brunches. My team and I were also the first to put together a ministry expo, highlighting the various ministries in the church. The skills I learned working in that environment would serve me well when I eventually ventured into my own business.

In 2012, things began to transition. The job I had been with for a few years shut down its Atlanta location. I took the severance package and decided not to get back into the workforce right away. There were a lot of meetup groups in the Atlanta area, and I became affiliated with one that was hosting an event on the "Mindset of a Millionaire." I figured it would be great to have that information, so I attended. After the presentation ended, there was an opportunity to join a network marketing travel business.

Although this experience was new to me, I was able to utilize my leadership skills to build a team. Through the weekly leadership training and quarterly boot camps, I learned how to posture myself and speak the language to attract other like-minded individuals. It was here that I heard the phrase, "the speed of the leader is the speed of the team." The famous quote was said by Lee Iacocca, the great American Ford Motor Company executive. He wanted to make sure his leaders were out in front, motivating their team to do better. I learned you have to walk with the walkers and run with the runners. Considering the speed of the team and adjusting accordingly, I was able to achieve success in this venture.

Throughout my network marketing experience, I received a lot of leadership training. One thing they emphasized was that leaders are readers. I was introduced to several books by

John Maxwell, who is noted as the world's most influential leadership expert by Inc. One of his quotes that stood out to me is, "Leaders must be close enough to relate to others, but far enough ahead to motivate them." He also said, "The true measure of leadership is influence – nothing more, nothing less."

These two thought principles stayed with me even after leaving network marketing to pursue my own businesses. I realized I had a passion for motivating and encouraging women, which led me into the field of women empowerment. I noticed, however, that when people thought about leadership, it was male dominated. The most famous leaders in history were Mahatma Gandhi, Nelson Mandela, Martin Luther King Jr, and other men. Mother Teresa was the only female privileged to be included.

That knowledge set me on a path to consider all of the women whose leadership skills and influence went under the radar. Those who sacrificed to make sure we survived. Those who risked their lives and reputations to pave the way for others to come behind them. Those who will never receive the recognition they deserve for all of the contributions they made to get women where we are today. Those who allowed women to stand on their shoulders to get close enough to break glass ceilings. These women are our unspoken heroes – our champions.

They say it takes a village; well, these women are our village. They paved the way for us to be leaders today. From our ancestors to those who participated in the fight for our equality, to those who instilled values in us as little girls or young boys, to those who taught us, coached us, or mentored us in some way, we must acknowledge their contribution to awakening the leader within.

I'm of the belief that all women are born to lead. We embody the confidence, courage, and compassion needed to be the true leader Douglas MacArthur referenced in the quote mentioned earlier. We inherently possess leadership characteristics that are stirred up from the womb. Our bodies are designed to produce life, which prepares us to be influencers of the life we carry. Women lead their child(ren) from infancy to adulthood without a roadmap. Urban.org featured an article that states that half of all households are now headed by women. They are stepping up to the plate and leading their families and are stepping out and leading in other arenas too.

In August 2020, I connected with a group of ladies to launch the SheEO District Community, led by its visionary and founder, Kellye A. Bowens. I am part of the Senior Leader Team as the Director of Senior Leader Development. The SheEO District is a multi-layered (health, business, wealth, social) super network of like-minded, purpose/goal-driven, self-motivated, progressive women from all around the world. Further, it's a synergistic merger of diverse gifts from all backgrounds joining positive energies to empower, inspire and ensure the success of our members from the starting point through the critical "Red Zone," where most tend to give up due to lack of motivation, support, and resources.

The opportunity to serve on SheEO District's leadership team has opened unlimited doors of opportunities both personally and professionally. I have had the pleasure of working with some of the most amazing ladies who have pushed me to be an even better leader. They have challenged and held me accountable to achieve goals I never thought were possible. In turn, I utilized the growth I experienced within the group to help other women in their personal and professional development.

It was my desire to give women a voice, see them speak their truth, and share their personal stories to empower others. That was the catalyst behind the anthology I wrote with 24 other ladies in December 2020 entitled, *I Am a Woman Empowered: Stories of Strength, Resiliency, & Triumphs.* Through this project, I recognized the power of unmuting your voice and telling your story. I saw the transformation within myself as well as the other ladies, and I knew I had found my niche.

Since publishing the book, I witnessed first-hand how powerful being an author can be. As I researched leaders in the literary field, it was inevitable that I would run across one of the most celebrated authors in the world, Toni Morrison. She was the first African American woman to win the Nobel Prize in Literature. Her writings were comprised of plays, children's books, and novels, earning her numerous prestigious awards such as the Pulitzer Prize and the Presidential Medal of Freedom from Former President Barack Obama. In 2000, Toni Morrison was named a Living Legend by the Library of Congress.

One of her most memorable quotes is, "If there's a book that you want to read, but it hasn't been written yet, then you must write it." President Obama called Toni Morrison a national treasure. Her body of work has inspired many writers to follow in her footsteps. Although she was a thought leader and change agent in the literary field, her impact went far beyond writing novels. She championed issues plaguing the African American community, helping to advance matters of civil rights and racial justice. She said, "If you are free, you need to free somebody else. If you have some power, then your job is to empower somebody else."

I knew helping others tap into their stories would open up doors of opportunity that could never be closed. Realizing the power of the pen, I launched A & M Publishing & Productions with my business bestie, Matthew Santana, Jr. Since the launch, we have helped more than 100 people become published authors, empowering them to tell their stories to make a difference in the lives of someone else.

In addition to publishing books, we also delved into publishing a digital magazine, iShine. When my business partner Rhonda Turner joined our team, we brought in contributing writers to highlight individuals who were shining in their business or career and making an impact in their communities. Our writers also provided content to help people shine mentally, spiritually, physically, as well as in their business or relationships. Our motto is, "When I shine, you shine; we all shine together."

The COVID-19 pandemic sparked what has come to be known as the "Great Resignation." In August 2021, I joined the crowd and made the decision to walk away from corporate America and pursue full-time entrepreneurship. It was a defining moment that awakened the leader within. I must say it has been an extremely rewarding experience. Leading a budding media company has increased my awareness of the influence I have and the responsibility that comes along with it. It is definitely not anything I take lightly. I recently enrolled back in school to take some classes to hone my skills even more. I believe leaders should be perpetual learners.

We are all born to lead. Whether you guide yourself or you're the leader in your home, office, business, or community, you must take steps to lead well. When you become a better leader, you become a better person. As you position yourself to step into the role of a leader, understand that people look towards leaders to take them to the best possible outcome. John Maxwell said, "Everything rises and falls on leadership."

I learned a few things that I hope will help you on your leadership journey.

1. **Lead yourself first.** Toni Morrison said, "You are your best thing." Leading ourselves well can be challenging. Oftentimes we run around trying to help others and put ourselves on the back burner. That type of action sometimes leads to anxiety, burnout, and possibly depression. We all have heard that you cannot pour from an empty cup. It's important to lead yourself first so that you are equipped to lead others.

2. **Lead with confidence.** There is no one on the planet like you, so be confident in the talents and skills you possess to lead others well. I'm not saying you will have all the answers because that's unrealistic. However, trust the process and move forward confidently, even if you have to do so afraid. I know that sounds contradictory, but don't allow fear to paralyze you. Allow your confidence to take over and walk in the expectancy that it will all work out fine!

3. **Leaders have a growth mindset.** John F. Kennedy said, "Leadership and learning are indispensable to each other." This type of mindset will serve you well in leadership. A growth mindset embraces challenges and believes anything is possible through study and learning. By

changing the way you think, you can change the way you learn and experience different results. You will begin to see failure as a natural part of the learning process. Challenges become opportunities for you to strive to become better every day.

    4. **Leaders have a vision.** Proverbs 29:18 says, "Where there is no vision, the people perish." There's no purpose or clear direction without an end goal in mind. Vision is vital for a leader because it provides inspiration and motivation to keep moving forward to achieve the goals at hand. The vision is a guide when challenges occur and serves as a strategic plan for success.

    5. **Leaders look for the win-win.** The definition of a win-win is a situation or outcome where everyone comes away happy. Leaders become intentional about negotiating from a mutual gains approach for the benefit of the team. "Teamwork is the ability to work together toward a common vision. The ability to direct individual accomplishments toward organizational objectives. It is the fuel that allows common people to attain uncommon results." ~ Andrew Carnegie

    6. **Great leaders are great communicators.** Effective communication is one of the most powerful tools a leader can have. Yet great communication isn't just about talking. The best communicators practice active listening and are excellent observers. They adjust their message to meet the needs and expectations of the people around them and can sense when the atmosphere shifts and pivot accordingly.

    7. **Leaders delegate authority.** No one should try to do everything themselves. Leaders who delegate authority empower their team, build trust and credibility, and help them develop personally and professionally. This gives

everyone a sense of value, allowing them to take ownership in the overall success.

    8. **Leaders are risk-takers.** Barry Farber said, "There's no reward in life without risk." Thomas Jefferson stated, "With great risk comes great reward." Leaders know they have to take risks to be innovative and on the cutting edge. Even in failure, they know they will walk away with more insight, knowledge, and experience, eventually leading to more success. The key, however, is to take calculated risks.

    9. **Leaders are agents of change.** They constantly think out of the box and often become pioneers, making an impact that goes beyond their lifetime. Leaders leave a legacy. They know the cause is bigger than them and implement actions to see it come to fruition. This is an exciting time for women because America has elected its first female Vice President, Kamala Harris. She is also the first African American and Asian American Vice President in history. Another first came from Ketanji Brown Jackson, who was confirmed as the first Black woman on the United States Supreme Court. These Black female pioneers are making phenomenal strides and breaking glass ceilings that previously only allowed us to watch the table but not have a seat at the table! God is doing a new thing. Revelations 3:8 (AMP) says, "I know your deeds. See, I have set before you an open door which no one is able to shut, for you have a little power, and have kept My word, and have not renounced or denied My name." It is a true testimony that no one can keep you from what God has purposed for you. He is the doorkeeper, and it is an open-door season for us all.

    10. **Leadership isn't a destination.** Leadership is a journey that includes highs and lows. As the world changes, you have to constantly evolve to adapt to it. Leaders are flexible and resilient. They bounce back from setbacks and, like diamonds, are defined by pressure.

Leadership is so essential, and I pray these 10 points have helped you in some way. Anyone can be a leader, but not everyone can be a great leader. In my favorite poem by Mariann Williamson, Our Deepest Fear, there's a part that says, "We were born to make manifest the glory of God that is within us. It's not just in some of us; it's in everyone." We are all born to lead. It is time to awaken the leader within and release the power we possess and leave our mark on the world!

BIOGRAPHY

Angela "ALove" Lewis is an Empowerment Speaker, Visibility Coach, and Publisher residing in the metro Atlanta area. Passionate about helping women use their gifts, talents, and voice, she guides their brands with proven strategies that provide the visibility and credibility needed for them to elevate and dominate in the marketplace.

Her desire to give women a voice and see them share their personal stories to empower others was the catalyst behind her anthology, I Am a Woman Empowered: Stories of Strength, Resiliency & Triumphs. Since publishing the book, Angela has assisted numerous others in publishing their work through A & M Publishing & Productions. She is editor-in-chief of the digital magazine iShine, a curated publication designed to highlight individuals making an impact in the community. In addition, she hosts two podcasts, iShine and Innervation: Motivating You From the Inside Out. Connect with Angela @iamangelalewis on all social media platforms or via her website at www.iamangelalewis.com.

"Don't sit down and wait for the
opportunities to come.
Get up and make them."
~ Madam C. J. Walker

WHAT DOESN'T KILL YOU …
REV. KEEVER LERNISE MURDAUGH

The phrase "What doesn't kill you, makes you stronger," is one that I have relied upon my entire life. It has helped to keep the issues of life into perspective. Nothing is as bad as it may seem, even when life is handing you weighted balls to juggle. There are always brighter days on the other side of darkness, but to enjoy the beautiful sunshine, sometimes you have to endure the storms.

There's no place like home…so I thought!
My earliest memories of home-life, unfortunately, were not good ones. In fact, I remember being very poor and it was an extremely hard situation. I have heard stories of children being poor but not realizing that their families fell below the poverty guidelines until they were adults. Well, that is not my truth. From my earliest memories of childhood, I knew we were poor. How did I make that correlation? Well, I knew by the soft spots and holes that were in the floors of our single-wide trailer, especially the one behind our kitchen sink under the kitchen window. I knew by the snake that my mother killed on our kitchen counter because it crawled into our house through that hole in our kitchen. I knew by the way my bed straddled the beam in the floor of my bedroom.

Any sudden move and the foot of my bed could have fallen in at any given moment.

I knew because we were reminded by others at school, family functions, and even at church. One of my aunts never passed up an opportunity to remind me and my sisters of how we had to wear clothes, or the $3 white canvas sneakers from Family Dollar, and how she was able to purchase clothes for her children from J.C. Penney and Belk. She would say things like, "Y'all are poor, and we are rich." Yes! We were poor and we were reminded of it every waking moment of our lives.

To add insult to injury, my father was extremely abusive, and he was a drunk. He was the epitome of a narcissist. Not only was he physically, verbally, and mentally abusive to my mother, but also to us as children. I remember as a little girl holding and comforting my two younger sisters at night when he and my mom would get into a fight. AND THAT SOUND; that sound of her body hitting the wall and hearing them rumbling and tumbling is something that still makes me cringe, even as a 44-year-old adult. If something falls around me that remotely sounds like that, my reflexes react immediately, and I stand still. It is something that I have not been able to shake even to this day.

I recall him leaving the house on the weekends and coming back home later at night or the following day extremely drunk and in a rage. We knew by the sound of his blue Ford pickup truck accelerating down the road to our trailer, that as soon as he got in the house, all hell was going to break loose. My sisters and I would try to help our mom, but as little girls, we didn't really know what to do. She would try to push us out the way so we would not catch those licks that he was handing down to her. Our mom was a trooper. I remember thinking that she was so brave yet so timid. I could not wrap my little mind around why she just would not leave him. Of course, me being a little girl, she did not share her thoughts with me. She did not share her fears, reservations, or uncertainties either. As hard as she tried, she could not hide the pain in her eyes, as well as the bruises that covered her face and body.

I imagine that she stayed because she knew that my sisters and me depended on her for survival. Working as a cafeteria staff member in an elementary school did not pay that much back then, especially if you did not graduate from high school. To say my mom did not finish high school, she was very cunning in a way. Because she learned and gathered strength from those beatings, late night rendezvous, and my father's threats to kill her, us and then himself, that she finally formulated a plan to leave him. We were now on the run, hiding from my father. I remember so clearly the night we left. It goes without saying that life as a child in our home was tough as we experienced many adversities.

A week or two prior to us leaving, my parents got into a huge fight. I remember him hitting her so hard that I could hear his fist connecting with her body all the way down the long hallway in our trailer. I was scared. I thought he was going to kill her that day. Like so many times before, he threatened to kill all of us, including himself. At that moment, she believed he was telling her the truth and said to herself, "You will never kill me and my children." If she had not planned to leave, we probably would not be here today.

So, she went into action and started packing little things of ours here and there to take to a friend's house. She packed clothes, blankets, and other things that she knew we would need and made several trips until she was finished. She was so smooth with it that we did not even notice that anything was missing. Then finally, we escaped.

It was a cool fall night. Our mom took me and my little sisters to the county fair. We had the best time of our lives. She let us get on all of the rides, play games and we even had a little fair food. She was very smart. She used the fair as her cover to escape with us. She believed that he was going to kill us all very soon and she was not taking any chances with our lives. After the fair, we climbed in our little Ford Fiesta and left for her friend's house, where we stayed for nine months until my mom was able to get a two-bedroom apartment of our own.

We stayed in the apartment for about six months, but feared the next-door neighbor was planning to break in and rape us, so we moved. We must have moved about five or six times from the time we left our childhood home, and some of the conditions where we moved to were worse than living at home, minus the beatings. My mom did the best she could with what she had. She was a proud woman. She never asked my dad for a dime, and she did not make him pay child support either. All she wanted from the divorce was us and her little Ford Fiesta so that is what she got. I wish I could tell you that she stayed gone from him forever, but she did not. She stayed away approximately four or five years before going back to him. Like many other women who return to their abusers, she hoped that he had changed. He came with empty promises that everything was going to be different, but we all knew better. She stayed with him another four or five years before leaving him for good.

Overcoming adversity...
I wasn't like most children growing up. I was an extremely bright child. Because of my advanced nature, I was often

misunderstood by my extended family. My aunts, uncles, and cousins teased me relentlessly and called me "crack" (intended to mean crazy or lacking a few screws in the head). I also stuttered terribly that validated their assumption of me. I could not talk without stammering over my words and because of it, I had anxiety about speaking publicly. I would use my middle sister as my mouthpiece until she got older then she refused to translate for me any longer. So, it was all up to me then. I was forced to find ways to overcompensate for my limited ability to speak clearly so I used my intelligence to get me through.

My mother did not finish high school, but she was determined to show us the value of education. She says I was the fast learner in our family. If she showed me something once, I was quick to catch on and imitate it. She recalls how I learned to crawl at two months old by grabbing onto the sheet of the bed and pulling myself toward the edge and walking by the time I turned six months old. While refusing to use my walker, she recollects me holding on to the edge of the heavy glass, oval shaped coffee table in the middle of our living room and taking steps around it until finally I just decided to let go and take that first step on my own.

Despite the things my mother went through as a young, abused woman, she prepared me well to start school. I learned how to read, write and count all before age three. She did such an excellent job with me that I was too advanced for head-start preschool and was even advanced for kindergarten because I "knew too much."

As an elementary, middle, and high schooler, I continued to excel in my studies. I maintained an A average throughout school. Everything I did, I did it with excellence. I remember my mother telling me that I could be anything that I put my mind to, and I believed her. I had family members who I envied because it just looked like they had the life that I always envisioned for myself, a loving and stable home, money, and nice things. As a kid from the outside looking in, they had it all. When I asked my mom why they were better off than we were, she would always say, "Keever, it does not matter when you get there or how you get there. When they look up at the finish line, they will see you there too. It is all about how you finish."

For some reason, that gave me courage and the will to succeed. I joined several clubs at school. I worked hard in my classes and joined and excelled in the Junior Reserve Officer's Training Corps (JROTC), where I became the Battalion Commander during my senior year of high school. Our JROTC team won many competitions under my direction. That is when I noticed my innate ability to lead and win. I desired to win and be successful at everything I attempted to do, because, in my mind, I had something to prove. I wanted to prove to myself and others that I deserved to be at that finish line with everyone else. I wanted to prove that although my journey included many obstacles and adversities, I was determined to be great.

Despite my family not understanding me, I was somebody. I knew once I got to high school that I was something special. I recognized that I possessed a desire to rise above my circumstances and that many were ready to follow me.

Breaking Free
Most leaders have innate attributes that drive them to be successful in their endeavors. I also believe that some are born to lead out of a will to survive; a will to be better than their circumstances. Then, there are those leaders like me who were faced with many oppositions and chose to have

a positive outlook on life. I know that I am a natural leader given that I have overcome homelessness, poverty, a lack of family support and being told by several people in my life to give up because certain things were out of my reach; but I still defied the odds. As described below in the poem by Dr. Maya Angelou, I decided to rise.

Still, I Rise
By Maya Angelou

You may write me down in history
With your bitter, twisted lies,
You may trod me in the very dirt
But still, like dust, I'll rise.
Does my sassiness upset you?
Why are you beset with gloom?
'Cause I walk like I've got oil wells
Pumping in my living room.
Just like moons and like suns,
With the certainty of tides,
Just like hopes springing high,
Still I'll rise.
Did you want to see me broken?
Bowed head and lowered eyes?
Shoulders falling down like teardrops,
Weakened by my soulful cries?
Does my haughtiness offend you?
Don't you take it awful hard
'Cause I laugh like I've got gold mines
Diggin' in my own backyard.
You may shoot me with your words,
You may cut me with your eyes,
You may kill me with your hatefulness,
But still, like air, I'll rise.
Does my sexiness upset you?

Does it come as a surprise
That I dance like I've got diamonds
At the meeting of my thighs?
Out of the huts of history's shame
I rise
Up from a past that's rooted in pain
I rise
I'm a black ocean, leaping and wide,
Welling and swelling I bear in the tide.
Leaving behind nights of terror and fear
I rise
Into a daybreak that's wondrously clear
I rise
Bringing the gifts that my ancestors gave,
I am the dream and the hope of the slave.
I rise
I rise
I rise.

Despite the pain and uncertainty I faced as a child, I tapped into my strength and rose over my circumstances. The phrase, what doesn't kill you, makes you stronger, has more than one meaning for me. The things that I have gone through were designed to strengthen me. God knew that I would be in a position to witness and counsel other women who had similar experiences as I did. Our tests and trials are not just for us. Our testimonies are to be shared to show others what they need to do to survive and that it can, in fact, be done. God gives his strongest soldiers the toughest tests. It is His way of conditioning us to be greater.

If you were an athlete, you can recall how your coaches ran you into the ground during practices. I used to play basketball in middle school, so I remember how we had to run drills, after drills, after drills. Our coaches made us run so many suicide drills and practice shots that I use to dream about basketball at night. They literally drilled those plays into our memory so we would be better prepared to meet any opponent that we faced.

Of course, we won many games, but we lost some too. The lesson is not all about the wins; but instead, it is about how we prepared to win. How are you conditioning yourself to win? Are you using your moments of weakness to become stronger? Are you speaking affirmations over yourself, your loved ones and your business endeavors? Are you keeping negative people out of your inner circles and surrounding yourself with those who will speak life into you and your visions? Are you allowing the fear of pivoting or adjusting limit you from progressing forward? Are you afraid to JUMP out of a fear of feeling imperfect?

If this is you, then I encourage you to rise above your fears, anxieties and feelings of inadequacy. You are more than a conqueror and your story needs to be heard. Despite my more than humble beginnings, being raised in an abusive home, being poor, homeless and having a speech impediment, I still rose. I was able to finish high school in the top 10 percent of my class, attend college majoring in physical therapy assistance, started several businesses, raised a family with a husband who lives with epilepsy, and mentor and coach other women how to do the same. I am strong, courageous, and relentless and it shows in everything that I do.

Your story is not just for you. It is to help others overcome rough spots along their journey and that they will come out victorious the same way you did if they don't quit. Do not be afraid to share it. Who knows, it just might save your life or someone else's.

My mother is one of the strongest women that I know. Despite being abused, having to fend on her own while working three jobs to raise me and my two younger sisters, all while having a limited education, she survived. She rose above her circumstances. I drew my strength from her. I used her life as a teachable moment of what I did not want to endure as an adult. During my youth, I made a conscious decision to make better choices in adulthood and to pattern my life in such a way that I would not have to endure what she did. That is truly learning from someone else's pain.

What doesn't kill me...
Now it's your turn to make it personal and fill in the blank. Say it out loud, "What doesn't kill me, makes me_____." . With everything I've endured, I chose to fill in the blank with words that describe who I am ... stronger, smarter, resilient, dependable, trustworthy, a fighter, a survivor, accomplished, courageous, bold, confident, beautiful and worthy. What God brought me to, He also took me through. Yes, I came out smelling like smoke sometimes, but I'm thankful that I do not look like what I have been through. I am still here, and I am here to win, and you can too.

BIOGRAPHY

Rev. **Keever Lernise Murdaugh** is an Executive Business, Automation and Media Specialist, and Leadership Development Coach from Camden, South Carolina. She helps leaders implement soft skills training and workshops and teaches them how to effectively introduce automated systems to improve profit margins, time management, and decrease stress levels.

In addition, she teaches her clients how to leverage their digital footprint to improve their credibility while maximizing their exposure and visibility. She's an entrepreneur and small business owner, a licensed physical therapy assistant, an international motivational speaker, a certified life and business coach, an ordained minister, an advocate and board member and a TV, podcast host, and producer of the #1 TV show and podcast "Keever's Place."

Her favorite scripture is Proverbs 3:6, "In all thy ways acknowledge Him and He will direct thy path." Connect with Keever @ Linktr.ee/KeeverMurdaugh and subscribe to her TV Show and Podcast on all digital platforms, Facebook, Instagram and YouTube @KeeversPlace.

"You are where you are in life because of what you believe is possible for yourself."
~ Oprah Winfrey

RESILIENCE AGAINST ALL ODDS
KEIAUNDRIA RAGLAND

Have you ever wondered why some people switch from job to job, career to career, or from one major to another? Maybe one had a passion or desire to become a nurse, but during preparation and testing, they came up short. Life forced them to take a different path, or they had to create a path of happiness in an area that gave them a reason to live and love life.

When thinking about awakening the leader within, understand that there are some abilities inherent in your DNA that's taken root and is waiting on you to water it. One of the most inspirational African American leaders in my life is Helen Wimberly, my aunt. She was born on December 27, 1943, and early on in her career, she attended nursing school, but unfortunately, when she sat for the board exam, she fell short by several points. As you know, nursing is not for the weak, not for one with a selfish heart, or who doesn't care about the health and welfare of others. Although my auntie missed the mark and did not become a nurse, what's inspiring about her story is that she did not allow her setback to stop her from caring about people, loving them from the bottom of her heart, or helping them in their time of need, often sacrificing her own. She was inspired and strengthened by and had the courage of her mother Mildred Elizabeth Ragland who was born in 1916. My Aunt Helen was determined more than ever to start a business of her own and she opened a daycare in the basement of her home in 1974. As she continued to press forward, sometimes against the odds, she successfully opened a second daycare and both are fully established in East Knoxville, Tennessee – ABC Kiddie Academy and East Knoxville Learning Center. She is Black History.

The moral of my introduction is no matter what, find resilience to keep hope alive during times of adversity. Awaken the leader in you because it exists. You have to develop it, nurture it, water it, and identify your why. What made you choose your current major, career, business, or ministry? When you're passionate about your choice, you won't allow anything or anyone to change how you feel or tell you it's impossible. You must strive and continue to work hard in order to build your faith and succeed. Success does not happen overnight. Great things take time. So keep pushing.

How does leadership affect me as a growing author, coach, and speaker? When the weight of trying to do it all gets heavy and the ability to hold it together becomes overwhelming, my desire to endure to the end won't allow me to quit. I've had to push myself when no one else would. At times, I had to remember the little girl in me who would lead with or without an audience, no matter if someone were watching or not, listening or not. My leadership qualities emerged around age 9 or 10. I had a vivid imagination and remember teaching my "imaginary students" in my bedroom ... my "classroom". I would walk up the steps at home pretending as if I were leading my students to class. I would say, "Come on class, everyone walk in a straight line."

In my room, I pretended assigning them seats and giving them their assignments. My mother would call me by my nickname and say, "Keke, who are you talking to?" I would say, "My classroom, momma." But I knew then, I had a voice and a gift to lead, and it was being shaped at that very moment.

Later, I found myself doing hair in my momma's living room, which didn't last long. If nothing else, I made a little money, while lending my ear to others who needed someone to talk to. However, I was distracted by other things and at that time it no longer was fun for me. You've heard the saying, "You can run but you can't hide?" Becoming a hairdresser may have not been my exact calling, but I keep finding myself in leadership roles and volunteering for assignments where I have oversight. It prompted me to become more aware of my leadership characteristics. I've been a cheerleader coach, choir director, Mary Kay Consultant, youth director, and owner of a medical scrubs business with no prior experience in any of these areas. I I've often asked myself how could this be? The Lord always shows me favor even when I don't understand why. One of my favorite sayings is, "The Lord won't put more on you than you can bear."

God guides us through many phases in life to be pruned, purged, shaped, and strengthened for future assignments, to bear more fruit, and to develop our gifts. I decided to accept and carry out those assignments because I care and did not want to pass up an opportunity to serve. There were many days when I felt anxious and doubted my ability to carry out the assignment. The Lord reminded me that what I was doing was to please Him and not man. I was not called to be popular or to be in the forefront to be seen. Sometimes we're called to work behind the scenes. The comfort in the call is to know that you were chosen by Him. The Lord will not let you be put to shame. Trust in the inner heart of your calling. Psalm 25:1-2 NIV, "To you, O Lord, I lift up my soul; in you I trust, O my God. Do not let me be put to shame, nor let my enemies trump over me."

Trust the process. Leading others has caused me to become INTENTIONAL about my career and business. Reflecting back on my Aunt Helen's story, don't let the world's "NO" keep you from accomplishing what you were created to do and who you were created to be. I wrote my first self-published book in 2018, never thinking that I would become an author. During a season of my life, I decided to journal. I was married and always desired marriage, but because of self-doubt and not realizing my worth, I didn't think it would ever happen. However, my faith increased. Through every experience, trial, and teaching moment, my character and confidence has flourished. During my journaling, the Lord told me to develop it into a book. Not knowing and understanding the publishing process, again, I questioned my ability. Journaling was one thing, writing a book was another. However, this anthology makes the third book that carries my name. Don't dismiss your small beginnings. During a particular time while I was in praise and worship God connected every dot. He connected me with the right people to network with. Word of wisdom: Sometimes we have to go out of our normal circle to get our needs met and to accomplish God's will. But sometimes your initial help is within reach, and you just have to ask God to open your eyes and show you who's willing to lend a helping hand. Everything concerning me, the Lord perfected.

"The Lord will vindicate me; your love, Lord, endures forever – do not abandon the works of your hands." Psalm 138:8 (NIV).

Not only am I an author, co-author, and faith-purpose coach, I, Keiaundria Ragland am Chief Executive Officer of She's Purpose Ke and am planning my first two-day revival and expo, "The POWER Moves H.E.R." I'm also a Registered Health Information Tech. The test required to achieve this certification was the hardest I've ever taken. The first time I sat for this exam was when I came out of college around 2004-2005. I failed it twice and the second time I missed passing it by ONE point. However, over the years, I had to work my way up, gain experience, and even change jobs. Because all promotion comes from the Lord, he lead the way. He challenged me in 2021 to try again. So I pushed past my fears and started studying. I became intentional and resilient against the odds. Through it all, I had to focus to retain new information, create a strong foundation from which to build on, go from being a procrastinator to purpose driven. A delay does not mean a denial. Life will throw you curve balls sometimes, but the leader in you must still push forward.

In the words of the late Maya Angelou, "You can't really know where you are going until you know where you have been." A legendary author, poet, activist, and all-around inspiring woman, her mission in life was not merely to survive, but to thrive; and to do so with passion, compassion, humor, and style. Reflecting on those who have gone before us gives us hope for today. It is an honor to be a part of this book project and among other Black women who desire to lead even in an era where the impacts of slavery, racism and discrimination are still evident today. Although we are living in perilous times, we still must believe in ourselves and persevere. We can't be afraid to take risks and continue to lead. Each one of us has a tolerance level where we sometimes feel that we can't go much further, but by faith, through Christ Jesus, we are able to go beyond our own capabilities.

Another great African American woman who exhibited great leadership was educator Nannie Helen Burroughs. Her life's work helped to lay the foundation for many of the successes Black Americans enjoy today. As women, I believe we can find similarities in her story. She exhibited exemplary leadership after being denied for a position she was more than qualified for. To add insult to injury, the denial came at the hands of those who looked like her. It was assumed that her complexion was too dark. One of Nannie Helen Burroughs's infamous quotes was, "If you can't find a job, make one." She took her own advice and did just that. She opened her own school despite being rejected and was successful in educating many! Now that's leadership. Burroughs was very aggressive. She learned how to tackle problems head on. Just like her, we were born to lead. Often times, the world's "no" leads us to God's "yes."

In conclusion, many of our blessings are in overcoming life's obstacles. Determination, resilience, and perseverance are a part of AWAKENING THE LEADER WITHIN. It may not always look or feel pretty, and sometimes comes with a lot of no's and disappointments. However, be encouraged in knowing that at the end of every tunnel is light. At the end of every rainstorm is a pretty rainbow or a beautiful sunrise. We may go from job to job, career to career, or through testing and failures. However, our experiences aren't meant to benefit just us, but to help somebody else. No one is an island. We all need help on some level and can't get to any place of significance without it. Learning in the most uncomfortable places develops character, leadership, and courage. Courage has helped to cultivate the leader within me as well as to make difficult decisions and to challenge the decisions or actions of others. It also has taught me how to engage the world around me, what to take notice of and what to reinforce, who to engage in conversation, what I value, what I choose to act on, and how to make informed decisions. Taking risks is inevitable and isn't always negative. Sometimes, it provides the most valuable business lessons an entrepreneur can learn. One thing I learned at the start of my entrepreneurial journey as a Mary Kay Consultant is that I had to think beyond what I could see. When buying products for my shelf inventory, I planned to have a set number of parties a month. At each party, I expected to have five to six faces and make sales. Even though I planned with high expectations to meet or exceed my goal, that was not always the outcome. What did that force me to do? Giving up was not an option, it was time to press my way through. It was time to engage potential clients in warm conversations and to let them know how I could serve them. I had to embrace my voice and understand that sitting in silence was not going to bring me more business. We have been called for a purpose and to walk in confidence with our head held high. There were times when I became weary, procrastination set in, and I would not move. I took the necessary time to re-examine my WHY. By doing so, I regained my traction and repositioned myself. In every season, life brings lessons, and when we learn from them, they turn into blessings. We must adapt to our circumstances and recover from our setbacks. By doing so determines our response. We fare better when we choose peace over anger, refrain from blaming others, and hold ourselves accountable for our actions. True leaders exhibit these actions and lead by example. Through introspection, sometimes, taking a break is necessary so we know how to proceed. Leaders also know the importance of extending grace to themselves. At times, we can be our own worst critic.

As I reflect on my Aunt Helen Wimberly, Nannie Helen Burroughs, Maya Angelou, and countless other African American women leaders, I'm reminded of just how strong I am. They faced and overcame various hardships. However, they remained optimistic and looked on the bright side in order to be an inspiration for those who would follow them by exhibiting perseverance, staying focused, and refusing to give up.

BIOGRAPHY

Keiaundria Ragland is an Author, Coach, Speaker, Event SWAG Bag Specialist, and is the Chief Executive Officer of She's Purpose Ke. Born and raised in Knoxville, Tennessee, her life's experiences have inspired her to write, encourage women, and become a certified life coach.

As a woman of faith, Keiaundria understands what it means to be determined and what it takes to persevere as illustrated in her first book, *Life At A Glance: Single, Married, Togetherness*, that she self-published in 2018. In 2019 her chapter, "Seeking the Father Figure "IN HIM"" was included in the anthology, *Meant For My Good,* so she's not a stranger to the publishing world.

Since the start of Keiaundria's publishing journey in 2018, she has developed two coaching programs – Empowerment Online Training: From Stress to Success and Reignite Your Passion Group Coaching Program: Healing from Burnout and Work Overwhelm. She has also been featured on the following podcasts, Hope-In-Christ, "Be Inspired with Ursula," "Never Be Afraid To Stand In Your Truth", "A KISS with A LOVE," as well as the front cover spotlight in New and Noteworthy Women's Enterprise Magazine, highlighted in FREE2BME Magazine, a nominee at the I Am H.E.R International Hybrid Women's Conference and Awards show, featured as a motivational speaker at the T-Tops Conference for Teen Girls, a speaker at the Queen's Round Table Quarterly Symposium with Realizing Your Potential LLC, and a broadcaster on Kingdom Purpose TV focusing on the topic, "Building Our Inner Strength."

Connect with Keiaundria on all social media platforms and you may also visit her website: shespurposeke.com.

"Every great dream begins with a dreamer. Always remember, you have within you the strength, the patience, and the passion to reach for the stars to change the world."
~ Harriet Tubman

THE ROAD TO CEO: OVERCOMING THE STORM

NATALIE S. WILLIAMS, ESQ.

Have you ever made a wrong turn in the middle of the night down a dirt road? I have and let me tell you it is not something that you want to do. I lived on a dead-end dirt road until I was almost 18 years old. Honey let me tell you, those roads are not smooth especially after a storm of any kind. No one wanted to drive down that muddy, bumpy, and rocky road. We often parked on the main road and walked the rest of the way after a bad storm because my father didn't want to get his "Nelly Bell" (78' Mercury Zephyr) or that 72' Mercury Monterey stuck in the mud. The road to CEO reminds me somewhat of that dirt road except it was hundreds of miles long and took nearly five years to travel. It was a lonely treacherous terrain with steep mountains and deep valleys. The weather I encountered on this journey was unpredictable as a hurricane with its aggressive rainbands, violent and destructive winds, calm, and peaceful center that was essentially life changing.

Hurricane season usually occurs between June 1 and November 30. During this timeframe warm air rises above the surface of the ocean causing low pressure below, ultimately creating a thunderstorm to form. In layman's terms, a hurricane is nothing more than a series of thunderstorms that combine to form one big super storm that rotates. It has three main parts (a) the eye, which is the calm center; (b) the eye wall, the most violent part where the winds and rains are the strongest; and (c) the rain bands; which spin out from the center giving the storm its size. Hurricanes are rated on a scale of 1 to 5, with 5 being the most severe.

Being from Eastern North Carolina, I have lived through my fair share of hurricanes. However, none of them were as severe as the hurricane my mother lived through as a child. On Oct. 5, 1954, Hurricane Hazel made landfall on the coast of North Carolina, the only Category 4 hurricane to hit Eastern North Carolina to date. My mother Rosa was 8 years old and lived in a small wood house with her mother, grandmother and seven younger siblings. She describes her house as a "raggedy wood house; that if you looked up you could see the stars; if you looked down you see the dirt; and if you looked to the left or right you could see the sunshine through the wood planks."

My mother described Hazel as fast moving with its violent winds blowing directly through the walls and the rain falling on her face. That was until a stillness came through that she describes as the calm after the storm. She went outside to look around and saw absolutely nothing; it was oddly quiet and peaceful. There were no clouds, wind, or rain. There were no birds in the sky and no animals moving about. You couldn't even hear the crickets she said. It was completely still. She later learned that she was in the "eye" of the storm. But it wasn't calm for long, lasting only about 30 minutes. My mother said the stillness turned into the calm before the storm.

The second half of Hazel was worse than the beginning she said. It felt like the storm was pulling the ground apart as the trees were being uprooted by the wind. The sounds of destruction were around them and she felt as if they were all going to die that day. After the storm ended, my mother and grandmother went outside to look around. The neighbors told my grandmother that they looked out their window waiting to see their house be destroyed and them killed by Hazel. Ironically, that raggedy wood house with its poor infrastructure was the very thing that saved their lives. God took the house's weaknesses and used it to protect the blessings inside.

The "hurricanes of life" occur when there is a shift in your atmosphere which creates a friction between who you were and who God called you to be. The atmospheric shift happens when you are obedient to the call on your life. That obedience activates your faith, which in turn changes your natural sight to the divine vision of God. This is what the Bible refers to as the season of seedtime and harvest.

My mother is quiet, strong, and humble with a smile that will light up any room. Everything that I learned about inner strength, reliance, perseverance, and faith; I learned by watching my mother, especially when she was quiet. But when she speaks it's with authority, truth, and love. If you do not want the truth, do not ask my mother. I guess that I where I get it from too. But the greatest lesson I learned from her is faith in God despite my circumstances. I can hear her saying, "Baby, the storms of life will come, but if you have God, ain't no devil in hell or on earth that can stop you."

The Formation

I entered a new season in my life when I got married. It was indeed a happy time, but I was having somewhat of an identity crisis. In a matter of minutes, 45 to be exact, after the wedding ceremony ended, the woman I knew for 33 years no longer existed. My entire identity changed. My title changed from Miss to Mrs. My middle name, the name my family called me was no more. My last name changed. I had to change my driver's license and social security card. I was no longer Natalie. I was "his wife." I felt a piece of me was lost, and no one understood why I was so bothered. And my husband was wondering why I couldn't "just be his wife."

I went to one of my church leaders for guidance on this issue. She posed the following question to me: What is the "more" that you want to be if you had no restrictions? At that moment, I felt this awakening in my heart, and knew that I was not walking in the calling that God had for me. I was walking adjacent to it, but not in it. I could no longer settle being a Probation/Parole Officer (PO) anymore; 12 years of chasing and arresting people was enough. God didn't call me to be a PO, He called me to be an attorney and it was time for me to walk in my calling.

For every action there is an equal and opposite reaction. Defined as Newton's Third Law of Motion, it proved to be true regarding the formation of the hurricane in my life. However, my obedience to my calling activated my faith causing a shift in the atmosphere. As God revealed to me who He had called me to be, my thinking changed causing me to rise above the water of my comfort zone; leaving the low pressure of who I was below. The friction in the atmosphere brought about the opposite reaction. The Bible says in Ephesians 6:12 "For we wrestle not against flesh and blood, but against principalities, powers, and rulers of darkness of this world." These opposing forces hated my obedience and faith and were determined to keep me from doing what God called me to do. As a result, all hell had broken loose and what felt like a Category 5 hurricane, who'll I'll call Tempest had formed.

Making Landfall

One Saturday morning while I was studying for the Law School Admissions Test (LSAT), the storm started brewing. The tension in the air was so thick you could cut it with a knife. A simple "no" to a question caused an eruption and the bottom to fall out of the sky. The deep roaring thunder shook the walls and caused the windows to rattle. The raging winds blew as my laptop flew across the room, hit the wall, and smashed into pieces. This storm was accompanied by an earthquake in my dining room measuring 3.0 on the Richter scale.

After it ceased, I surveyed the damage to my home. I cried in terror and confusion as I stepped over glass, wood, and drywall from the holes left in the walls by the storm's rage. Thankfully, I fled to my parents to safety given that I had never experienced anything like that before in my life. Ironically, Hurricane Irene was making landfall on the shores of Eastern North Carolina at the same time the Category 1 storm Abaddon had left my home.

Remembering my mother's advice to keep some of my personal issues to myself, I shared very little of what happened with my parents out of fear of retaliation. Where did this storm come from? I had no clue, but what I did know was that God would not put more on me than I could bear. I had to keep my eyes on Him and not Abaddon, or I'd sink like the Disciple Peter did in Matthew 14:22-32. After Hurricane Irene had lost her strength, I returned home and surprisingly it had been cleaned and the damage to the walls and furniture repaired.

The Eye

My mother always said, "Every closed eye ain't sleep, and every goodbye ain't gone." As a kid, I never knew what that truly meant, but soon learned. Things had quieted down, and it reminded me of what my mother often referred to as the calm before the storm. After I took the LSAT in November the tension I had felt previously had softened. But by the end of December, it had returned and became more intense like a dense fog. I found myself becoming more and more annoyed by the day and was so exhausted I began falling asleep while sitting at a stop light. Everything had come to a head on December 23rd. This time it wasn't a simple "no" that caused the problem, it was my response, "are you serious" that caused the rain and winds to return to return with a vengeance. However, I had made up my mind that I was done going through these bi-polar storms and was fed up with being emotionally drenched by its rain.

I called my friend from church to share with her how I was feeling, and she came over to visit me. Because she felt that my emotions had been all over the place she thought I might be pregnant and brought a pregnancy test over with her. When she pulled it out, I said to her, "Really ... you just happened to have a test in your purse?" However, I appeased her, took the test and went to the mailbox to retrieve my mail. Inside the mailbox were my LSAT scores and a conditional acceptance letter from a law school in Georgia. Excited, I came back into the apartment and there was my friend standing and smiling from ear to ear. I said to her, "I told you I wasn't pregnant." Then I looked at the test and saw those two blue lines.

Overwhelmed can't begin to explain how I was feeling. I couldn't believe I was pregnant. I said, "Really God, this is not the time to play games with me. What about law school?" I was not ready to be a mother. I didn't want to be a wife anymore. I had already planned to pack up my things in a U-Haul and leave the pregnancy test on the table with separation papers. However, my friend convinced me otherwise. She said that my feelings at the time more than likely were hormonal as a result of being pregnant. With a due date of late August, there was no way I could begin law school that year. It would not have been a good look going into labor while in class.

However, as my belly grew bigger and bigger, so did my anxiety about motherhood and law school. Every day I waddled to the mailbox and waddled back with another rejection letter. When I had gotten the 10th one, I told my husband that I thought it was time for Plan B. So, I enrolled in graduate school to study Clinical Health and Counseling. I had convinced myself that maybe law school wasn't what God wanted for me and my time had passed. Nevertheless, I knew He had a plan and I continued to speak faith, even though I had begun to question my calling.

In March of 2013, I received an unexpected call from a prominent law school in the Midwest offering me a seat in their upcoming 1L class. I hadn't applied to this school, nor had I even heard of it. The admission's office waived my application fee and asked me to send my documents right away. They said because there had been a technicality with my application to expect my acceptance letter within two weeks. However, two months had passed before it actually happened. Then they hit me with the double whammy that I needed to pay the $500 seat deposit to hold my spot within a week.

As a woman faith I believe in the power of prayer. So I made my request known and prayed, "God, I need $500 by

Friday to go to law school if this is your will for my life." The next day I went to the mailbox only to find a letter with a check attached for $512 from a closed account during my undergraduate studies that I'd forgotten about. The July after my 35th birthday we packed up our son and moved to the Midwest. Everything seemed perfect. I was finally going to do what God called me to do, my son was healthy, and my husband had found a new job there before we moved. Peace had finally arrived, or so I thought. Again, I remember what my mother had previously shared with me.

The Eyewall
This is the part of the hurricane that meteorologists say is the worst. This is where the winds are the strongest and the rain is the heaviest. This is where major destruction takes place. It was no different with my hurricane either as all hell had broken loose during my first semester of law school.

I bore the weight of my world on my shoulders and was sinking like quicksand. Nothing I did or said was right. Continually, I was accused of being "fake." However, if I did nothing, the perception was "I didn't give a damn." It was damned if I do and damned if I don't. I struggled as I juggled being a full-time wife, mother, and student without any family support. I barely functioned on four hours of sleep a night and three, 24-ounce cups of coffee a day. There were more bills than money; robbing Peter to pay Paul then robbing Paul to pay Peter trying to survive on one income and student loan refund checks.

In addition to everything else, racial tension spread throughout the law school and the surrounding community as my 1L class was the most racially diverse class the law school had ever seen. It was almost like the days of Jim Crow that my parents use to tell me about. Specifically, when the schools began to integrate. It was them against us. We were profiled daily by police, refused service at restaurants and stores, and experienced price gouging for rent. A noose was even hung outside of the law school and me and my fellow Black classmates were often told to go back to where we came from. All the while, some of the professors made jokes saying the 1L class were products of the No Child Left Behind initiative.

My skin is the color of dark chocolate, and my last name is sweet like confections; yet my professor felt it was appropriate to call me "Hershey" to remember my name. A Southern belle like me, stuck out like a sore thumb in the Midwest. The simplest hello stopped people in their tracks wanting to hear me speak the more. But my writing professor referred to my Southern dialect and drawl as "ignorant" and recommended that I change who I was to "fit in" with the likes of them. To add insult to injury, I was one of many women of color who had big, beautiful natural hair. We were denied internship opportunities and told to straighten our hair to be a proper candidate for certain law offices and judicial internships.

To top it off, I failed Torts, one of my required courses. As I was crying, I heard a faint laughter and noticed a smirk, followed by, "It's about time you failed at something, now you know how it feels." I had to pray, "Lord help me not shank this n***** in his sleep." I told myself, "Keep your eyes on God, failure is not an option." As it turned out, there was an error with the grading system in the registrar's office. I actually got a B in the class. Thank you, God!

The stress of financial instability was growing during my 2L year, and an unnerving pattern of destructive winds and aftershock trimmers ripped through every part of my home. Depression fell like a weighted blank making it hard to get out of bed. As much as depression wanted me to lay next to it in bed for days to have a pity-party; I could not lay there waiting for God to answer my prayers. I could hear my parents saying, "God helps those who help themselves." Is that Biblical? I don't know. But I do know, "Faith without works is dead" (James 2:17 NKJV) is. So I swallowed my pride and applied for public assistance. This act of faith released finances to put food on the table and medical insurance for me and my son.

Tempest was so enraged by my continued faith and fight, that she released another storm called "Assassin." Assassin was determined to kill me by any means necessary. The surges of rain flooded me with tension, anger, frustration, anxiety, and depression. I was being ripped apart like a rag doll between two pit bulls and I couldn't take it anymore. Like before, I started to zone out while I was driving; having thoughts of running my car off the road or driving into a Mack truck on several occasions just so I could be free. But the sound of my son's cry or giggle in the backseat snapped me back into reality. Looking at his little handsome face reminded me that I had too much to live for and I couldn't leave him for the hurricane to consume.

I was weakened by Assassin's attempts on my life. I was alive but not living, I was merely existing and still battling with the constant winds and rains of depression that continued to pour. I decided to seek therapy. Assassin then turned its focus on killing my purpose. One night before my Trust and Estates final, my sleep was disrupted by a sudden downpour followed by violent winds, trimmers, and thunder. My refusal to acknowledge it only intensified its aggression. Can you imagine lying in bed praying to yourself to remain calm and then you feel your bed lifting off of the ground, followed by you flying into the wall.

The next morning the house was lifeless and cold. My refusal again to acknowledge Assassin's furry caused it to re-emerge destroying almost everything in its path leaving me without a phone to even call for help. And just like that, it was over, and the house was quiet again while I looked around to assess the damage. Devastated, exhausted, and in pain I gathered my belongings and headed toward campus.

As I was driving to take my exam, I called my mother. She could hear the pain in my voice, but when she asked me what was wrong, I said, "It's going to be ok." My mother replied to me like she had on so many occasions before, "Baby give it to Jesus and don't pick it back up again." After my exam, with puffy eyes and a swollen wrist, I met with the Dean to withdraw from school. However, she refused to accept it. I looked at her confused, and said, "I can't do this anymore, being a wife, a mother, and a full-time student." The Dean, who was this confident, feisty, white woman looked me in the face and said, "I will not accept this withdrawal form. I have seen so many students come into this law school because their parents heavily influenced them, or they were trying to find themselves. But you have a calling on your life to be an attorney and I refuse to let you quit. You are not on this journey alone." At that very moment believed God was not listening and was not there, yet at that very moment He was closest to me. God was moving the hearts of strangers and putting them in place to support me when I needed it most. He was dispatching his angels to fight and clear my path making this bumpy road smooth. Then I was able to see that God had placed anchors all around me to hold me down during this storm. I had classmates who were my prayer partners. I even had one who became like a "sister" to me and a Godmother to my son and watched him while I did laundry and hugged me when I cried. There were those who watched my son in the library while I took my exams. Others encouraged me to smile and to never dim my light. There was even one who bought me an apple pie a la mode when I sat in my car and cried. There were also those who became my pseudo family and my home away from home.

When it Rains it Pours
I come from a family of singers and musicians. You could not be in our house and not hear someone singing or playing an instrument. I learned early as a child, that when I felt discouraged, music was something that I could turn to that would give me peace and remind me that I was not alone. I remember how my father and I used to sing the song, "When It Rains It Pours," by Rev. F.C. Barnes and my mother was right there singing in harmony, "Storm clouds rise and billows roll, just seek Jesus and he'll bring sunshine, I'm so glad that Jesus knows."

That song is on point when it comes to life's hurricanes. Knowing that storms don't last forever, we often let our guards down. But again, I was reminded of one of my mother's favorite sayings, "Every closed eye ain't sleep and every goodbye ain't gone." Unfortunately, another hurricane hit. This storm was the master manipulator as it dumped insecurity, low self-esteem, and a low self-image fueled by an ultimatum to quit law school or lose everything. However, refusing to accept it; I stood in my T-stance ready to fight for my destiny. The storm reduced to a gentle breeze breathing fear and intimidation over me, leaving me with assured anxiety that because of my refusal to quit, my life was about to become a living hell.

I love the holidays, but after the last storm, every major family holiday that followed ended in depression and tears. Feelings of rejection, hatred, and unworthiness engulfed me, making what should have been a joyful day full of sorrow. Nevertheless, the song "Encourage" by Donald Lawrence played on repeat each morning as I prayed and reminded myself to keep my eyes on God, rather than focusing on the hurricane that was swirling around me.

My 3L year flew by and it was time to step my confessions of faith up a notch. Every Sunday during this year, I wrote on the back of my tithing envelope, "I am a first-time bar passer, 264, failure is not an option." I changed my computer screen to read, "264 first-time bar passer." I even had sticky notes all over my books, car, bathroom, and anywhere else I could think of. The Bible says in Habakkuk 2:2-3, "Write the vision and make it plain."

The hurricane became weak when I presented my graduate thesis on "The Psychology Behind Picking the Perfect Jury" and had the opportunity to test my theory the following spring as I sat 2nd Chair for a Murder Trial as a Certified Law Clerk with the Public Defender's Office. Lead Counsel, JP used my theories and questions during jury selection. All we needed was a hung jury and that was considered a victory for the defense. After eight and a half hours of deliberation, the jury advised the judge that they were deadlocked and couldn't reach a verdict, resulting in a hung jury. This was the confirmation I needed to remind me that God called me to practice law.

Just when I thought I could breathe and see the light of day, it was like Tempest turned left and went back out to sea to gain more strength. As my mother told me many times, it was another reminder that "Every goodbye ain't gone." This time, the storm come back to test my character and fitness. I completed my bar application and was scheduled for my Character and Fitness Interview with a local attorney. I was required to know the rules of professional conduct as an attorney and had to provide my complete credit report for review. I interviewed with a prominent White law firm not far from the law school. I was asked about my years of service in law enforcement and my decision to attend law school. But the tension increased as he meticulously reviewed my credit report. He asked me about every delinquent payment, charge off, and settlement on my credit report for over an hour.

I was nervous and sweating like a "hooker in church" as my grandmother used to say. Finally, after he was done reviewing my report, he asked me, "How can you be fit to practice law when you are not financially fit to maintain your bills?" I swallowed my pride, because what I wanted to do was curse him up one side and down the other. Hearing my mother say, "It will be ok baby, what God has for you is for you ... besides, one monkey don't stop no show." I explained to him that prior to my first year of law school, I didn't have any delinquent accounts and I had no credit cards. I showed him in my report that all the delinquent accounts were a result of unpaid medical bills. After several more minutes of explaining myself, he decided to approve me to sit for the bar exam.

However, later the next day, I received a voicemail from that same attorney saying he was rescinding his approval and was referring me to the character and fitness review board with the Board of Bar Examiners at the State Capitol later the next week. I was highly upset! That White man, who never had to work for anything in his life, and whose parents' paid his law school tuition had the nerve to tell me that I was not fit to be an attorney because I chose to have food, clothing, and shelter for me and my son rather than pay a medical bill. Sadly, I was not the only one he had denied. He had a prior track record denying several Black law students for character and fitness citing the same reasons he had given me. However, he approved one of my White classmates that was arrested for dealing marijuana while we were in law school and the felony charge was still pending. Yet, I was the one who was unfit and had poor, moral character.

It's not what they call you, it's what you answer to, my mother told me. My husband and I drove three hours to the State Capitol for my character and fitness hearing. The Board was comprised of about 10 people who were seated at a horseshoe-shaped table. I had to sit in a single seat at the bottom of the horseshoe facing them. I was "sweating bullets." There was only one person of color on the panel, and she looked at me with a calming smile as I took a deep breath before I introduced myself. Only one panelist grilled me like a homicide detective interviewing a suspect. He was loud and antagonistic as he sat on the edge of his seat. He was so rude and disrespectful. I tried to remain calm and explained to the entire Board the same things I had explained the week before. All of the other panelists seemed understanding of my situation being a nontraditional student trying to survive without much assistance from my family. However, he would not let it go. I blurted out in frustration, "I have been poor my entire life and I have never stolen a dime. My parents worked factory jobs making minimum wage to support us and we didn't steal from anyone ... nor asked for a handout ...we simply made do. I was a law enforcement officer for more than a decade where I dealt with gang bangers and drug dealers. If I wanted to steal, I could have, but my integrity is worth more to me than a dollar." But God always has a ram in the bush. The Head of the Board asked him to be quiet and that was enough. She looked at me and said, "I am impressed by you. You are married, have a toddler, and received a dual degree in law school, plus you have secured a good job prior to the bar exam. I am impressed." She asked me to go out of the room and wait while they decided on whether or not to approve me to sit for the bar exam.

So I exited the room and was seated in a small office the size of a closet. I was only out there for five minutes when the Head of the Board told me that I was approved and deemed fit to sit for the bar exam. She told me to never question my fitness as an attorney because I handled myself exceptionally well against a hostile group.

The Rebuke
In the Book of Matthew, Jesus rebuked the storm and it immediately ceased. My graduation day finally came and all of my family and closest friends where there to celebrate with me. Jesus heard my prayers in my prayer closet and sent a strong rebuke to the raging Tempest to cease and be still. Immediately I felt a sense of peace in the atmosphere. For the first time since the beginning of law school I was able to study without Tempest and her legion of hurricanes dumping all types of bi-polar weather fronts on me.

On July 26th, my 38th birthday, I walked into that Convention Center proclaiming, "I am a first-time bar passer. Failure is not an option; 265; and no weapon formed against me shall prosper." I laid hands on my seat and every seat surrounding me. I prayed that God would bring us peace and that we would all pass the July 2016 Bar Exam. Results came in the Friday before Labor Day weekend. I took a deep breath as I opened my email. I took an even-deeper breath as I read, "We are pleased to announce..." That is all I read! I fell to my knees thanking God and hugging my son.

After the calls of congratulations ceased and the house was quiet, the Tempest appeared looking confused, and his eyes were lifeless and empty. He said, "How did you pass after everything I did to you. You should have failed?" I smiled and said, "It was JESUS!"

The Blessing in the Hurricane

The malicious and violent intent of this Category 5 Hurricane was to destroy and kill the woman God was calling me to be. However, the only damage it caused was to itself. My mother always said, "The ditch you dig for me will be the grave you dig for yourself."(Proverbs 26:27 AMP) The blessing in all of this, is God will isolate you to reveal your destiny and/or hinderances in your life. He used the storm to detach everything that attached itself to me because a broken covenant. I had to go through it so that I could achieve my purpose in Him and to encourage others in similar situations.

I forgave everyone who played a part in the hurricanes of my life, whether it was done directly or indirectly. Each hurricane was necessary as it exposed character flaws in those I needed to cut out of my life, because they didn't recognize what I carried. Pastor John Gray said it best, "People will treat you like you are common, when they do not know what you carry... nothing exposes character more than a person who thinks they don't need you." I am blessed because every storm brought greater challenges resulting in a greater testimony. The opposition I faced was just confirmation of my promised destiny. My pastor says, "There is no victory without opposition." I am thankful to God for calling me into greater because He created me to be great.

As my mother Rosa used to say, "I do not have a mediocre child." Greatness is a choice; it is not by chance.

The storms of life will come. You will not get a warning from the weatherman, and you can't go to the hardware store to get boards to protect yourself. Nevertheless, the Bible says to stand against the wiles of the devil, you must put on the whole armor of God: the breastplate of righteousness; sword of the Spirit; feet shod (wear shoes) with the preparation of the gospel of peace; the helmet of salvation; the Shield of Faith; girding your loins with truth (Eph. 6:11-18 KJV).

The bigger the vision, greater is the storm; but there's no devil in hell or on the earth that can stop you. Remember these four key words: (1) Obedience, (2) Faith, (3) Resilience, and (4) Perseverance. It is in your obedience to your calling that your faith is activated and aligns your focus on God. It is your resilience that fuels the flames of your purpose through perseverance. The only thing that can keep you from being who you are called to be is YOU. The road to CEO can be treacherous, but you have what it takes to become a Confident Educated Overcomer because you are more than a conqueror.

The Posture of Leadership

Inquiring minds may want to know what any of my story has to do with leadership. It's quite simple. Leadership is a quality that is birthed through adversity. The hurricanes of life are labor pains designed to slowly stretch you past your comfort zone into a position to push out the purpose inside of you. Every test, trial, storm, and hurricane come to stretch us to a new level. However, it's not easy. Growing pains hurt but are worth it. It's amazing how women give birth after hours of intense labor and then forget all the pain they endured the very moment they look into their baby's eyes for the first time. The blessing is far greater than the pain we endured.

Life's hurricanes produce two types of people: (1) victims – those who succumb to the storm and (2) survivors – those who push through the storm. Survivors and leaders are the same, as they choose resilience and perseverance until the end. Google defines resilience as "the capacity to recover quickly from difficulties, toughness." It also defines perseverance as "persistence in doing something despite difficulty or delay in achieving success." To be a leader, you must be a survivor recovering quickly from difficulties and being persistent and patient until the end. In the words of the singing group, Destiny's Child: "I'm a survivor, I'm not gon' give up, I'm not gon' stop, I'm gon' work harder; I'm a survivor, I'm gonna make it, I will survive, keep on survivin'" "The race is not given to the swift nor the battle to the strong, but to the one who endures to the end." (Ecc. 9:11 and Matt. 24:13)

Another key trait in leadership is humility. "If you are the smartest person in your group, then you need to find a new group!" A quote from my two best friends from college. Everyone needs a mentor. They are not just for troubled persons. They exist to guide mentees on the path they are trying to go. You cannot be a leader if you cannot follow. You cannot lead if you do not know the way. How can the blind lead the blind? Someone must show you the way. After you have learned the way, it's now your responsibility to show someone else. When a leader has a mentor and mentee, it keeps them humble. When I was in my 3L year, my mentor was JP. I called her at least 20 times a day if not more. I was hungry and eager to learn from her because she was where I wanted to be. Every opportunity I had to learn from her in any form, I took it. Then it quickly became my turn to be the mentor to a mentee, passing on the skills I learned in and out of the courtroom as an attorney, a woman, a Black woman, and a Black female attorney in a field that is still made up of predominately white males.

To maintain a mentor/mentee relationship, one must also lead by example because someone is watching you. I am who I am because of the example my mother is for me. She is quiet but speaks volumes in her silence. She was a hard and dedicated employee. She never complained about the long hours or the pay. She never called off pretending to be sick. I honestly do not recall her ever missing work for herself. She worked her job and someone else's' if it needed to be done without being asked. Her mentality was if that assembly line had to keep moving, then she did whatever was necessary to make it happen. She cooked home cooked meals nearly every day because my dad didn't eat leftovers except on holidays. She attended my every band concert, parade, competition, game, doctor's appointment, and parent teacher's conference. She does not leave the house with her hair in bonnet, slippers on, hair rollers visible, or in a robe. She always greets everyone with a smile, love, and respect. She has a giver's heart and a praise of thanksgiving on her lips every day. I learned how to pray and speak over myself from my watching my mother. I learned how to smile and dance while enduring adversity by watching her dance on Sunday morning. I knew what a good wife was by watching my mother be a good wife to my father. I learned how to mother my son from the lessons I learned from her. My mother is my example of true leadership.

The final character trait of a good leader is the ability to forgive. Unforgiveness is a seed that will choke your growth. Forgiveness is not for the individual who wronged you; it is for you. If you hold unforgiveness in your heart against someone, that person will always have power over you. Unforgiveness is emotional slavery. However, forgiveness is freedom. I have gone through a series of counseling sessions in my life where forgiveness was always a discussed. I thought I had forgiven the individuals used by the storm, but I hadn't. I had to own the fact that during my ordeal I went into a state of survival mode and emotionally checked out to preserve my mind and heart. Nevertheless, after countless hours of intensive therapy in conjunction with prayer, I was able to release the pain and forgive; remembering what the Bible says, "for we wrestle not against flesh and blood...."

When you are in a leadership role of any faction, it is not done in isolation. There is no such thing as a leader of one. You must learn to co-exist with those that you disagree with, do not like, and those who have caused you nothing but turmoil. Dealing with difficult people is necessary to achieve a collective goal. Forgive them and be unbothered. I'm reminded of the following lyrics by Rev. Milton Brunson, a sweet song of freedom that simply says, "I'm free, praise the Lord I'm free, no longer bound, no more chains holding me, my soul is resting, it's just a blessing, praise the Lord, Hallelujah I'm free."

When you are in a leadership position, there will be countless people who will support you and countless people who will undercut you. They will smile in your face and stab you in the back. Don't hate them. Pray for and forgive them. There are no leadership positions where you lead in isolation. You must learn how to co-exist and work with people who have mistreated you. Haters have a place in our lives. They are necessary. If we didn't have them, then no one would even know how good we actually are at what we do. Haters bring attention to us. They provide the pressure we need to transform us from being ordinary to extraordinary, like diamonds.

In closing, the life we live will have tests, trials, storms, hurricanes, and some rare instances a Fujiwara effect, but know it is nothing you cannot conquer. It is the pressure that is applied to our lives in these difficult times that is needed to transform us from the ordinary to the extraordinary.

Do you know why diamonds are so precious? Because a diamond is an ordinary carbon whose molecular structure has been transformed into a crystal after being subjected to extreme heat and pressure. True leaders are diamonds also because they are ordinary people whose life's circumstances have transformed them into extraordinary beings by surviving extreme heat and pressures from the storms of life. Leaders don't just survive, they thrive. There is a leader in you ready to be born. It will not be easy. But trust God throughout the process. Be resilient, flexible, and adaptable. When adversity strikes, persevere, remain humble, free, and watch the C.E.O. be birthed out of your next hurricane.

BIOGRAPHY

Natalie S. Williams is a Southern belle, Mother, Attorney, Adjunct Professor of Criminal Justice and Psychology at the Indiana Institute of Technology, Pop Warner Football Team Mom/Coach, and above all a woman of faith from Merrillville, Indiana. She is a "Type-A/Over Achiever" that is the epitome of strength, resilience, and perseverance. She believes greatness is not by chance; greatness is a choice. Natalie uses this premise to challenge her nontraditional students to dream beyond their current circumstances. Even though her career is adversarial in nature, she hates to argue.

As a recent COVID survivor, she cherishes every breath and refuses to waste it. She has been known to say, "If you want me to argue outside a court of law, then you need to pay me a retainer." She is a confident, educated overcomer.

Connect with Natalie on LinkedIn and Facebook at Natalie S. Williams; Instagram: Freedom91919 or Clubhouse: natalieceo.

CONCLUDING THE WHOLE MATTER
JACQUELINE KABA-HARRISON

You were BORN TO LEAD and don't let anyone tell you differently! As African American women we come from a rich lineage of warriors and leaders. The ability to lead is a gift that has been passed down from generation to generation. Now, how you decide to nurture this innate skillset will determine the trajectory of your life.

Leadership is not new to us, from managing households to overseeing empires. Pause and think about the experiences in your life when you successfully lead an event or project that was thrown your way. Consider those accomplishments as stamps of approval and encouragement to continue leading those who are in your sphere of influence and beyond.

For those of you who grew up being told to be seen and not heard, I challenge you to stand up, speak up and accept your leadership crown. Others are looking to you for leadership, guidance, direction, advisement, accountability, and support. However for whatever reasons, you might feel reluctant to walk in your God-given roles because it's new territory. But I encourage you to take the first step and do it anyway, even if you have to do it afraid.

For those of you who were mislabeled, put it into perspective, consider the source, and remember that it's not what you're called, but what you answer to. There's a leader waiting to be awakened on the inside of you. She's been sleep long enough!

www.ingramcontent.com/pod-product-compliance
Lightning Source LLC
Chambersburg PA
CBHW071900070526
44583CB00016B/1779